THE
BOSTON
CELTICS
A CHAMPIONSHIP TRADITION
Fifty Years

"When it comes to tradition in basketball,
there are the Boston Celtics and there is everyone else."
BOB RYAN

THE BOSTON CELTICS

A CHAMPIONSHIP TRADITION

Fifty Years

By George Sullivan

Photography by Steve Lipofsky
and Dick Raphael

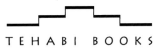

TEHABI BOOKS

The Boston Celtics: Fifty Years was conceived and produced by the Boston Celtics and Tehabi Books.

The project team from Tehabi Books included: Nancy Cash–*Managing Editor*; Andy Lewis–*Art Director*; Sam Lewis–*Art Director*; Tom Lewis–*Editorial and Design Director*; Sharon Lewis–*Controller*; Chris Capen–*President*. Additional support for *The Boston Celtics: Fifty Years* was provided by Steve Lipofsky–*Photo Editor*; Bill Center–*Copy Editor*; Anne Hayes–*Copy Proofer*; and Dick Johnson (New England Sports Museum)–*Technical Editor*. And from the Boston Celtics: Mark Lev, Jeff Twiss, David Zuccaro, and Jo O'Connor.

For more information on *The Boston Celtics: Fifty Years*, including corporate customized editions, please contact: Chris Capen, Project Director, Tehabi Books, 13070 Via Grimaldi, Del Mar, California, 92014, 800/243-7259.

Tehabi Books, in association with The Basic Foundation, a not-for-profit organization whose primary mission is reforestation, will facilitate the planting of two trees for every one tree used in the manufacture of this book.

Library of Congress Cataloging-in-Publication Data

Sullivan, George, 1933–

The Boston Celtics fifty years : a championship tradition / by George Sullivan : photography by Steve Lipofsky, Dick Raphael.

p.   cm.

"Preface by George Plimpton"—Jacket.

ISBN 1-887656-06-5. — ISBN 1-887656-07-3 (pbk.). — ISBN 1-887656-08-1 (leather)

1. Boston Celtics (Basketball team)—History. 2. Boston Celtics (Basketball team)—Pictorial works. I. Title.

GV885.52.B67S85   1996

796.323'64'0974461—dc20   96-32258

CIP

96 97 98 99 TBI 10 9 8 7 6 5 4 3 1

This edition is printed on acid-free paper that meets the American National Standards Institute Z39.48 Standard.

Printed in Hong Kong through Mandarin Offset.

PRECEDING PAGES: **T**he Celtics have given Boston plenty of opportunities to celebrate over their first-half century. It became a tradition for joyful fans to flood onto the parquet after championship-clinching victories at Boston Garden, such as this scene from 1986 (pages 2-3). The Celtics celebrate their first Eastern title en route to their first world championship in 1957 (page 4). Brent Musberger interviews Auerbach following the Celtics' 16th NBA title in 1986 (page 5), after which the party takes to the street for the traditional victory parade (page 6-7). The run of NBA titles began in 1956-57 with the team quarterbacked by Bob Cousy (page 8). The dynasty reached its peak in 1986 with the team led by Larry Bird, Kevin McHale and Robert Parish—a club that ranks among the best in NBA history (page 9). The Celtics' championship tradition is being carried into the new FleetCenter (page 10-11). At the heart of it all, at centercourt, is the most recognizable logo in the National Basketball Association—the jaunty leprechaun designed by Zang Auerbach (page 12).

CONTENTS

MY TEAM

BY GEORGE PLIMPTON

I have had an ongoing love affair with the Boston Celtics ever since I played briefly with them in one of my participatory journalistic stints back in 1969. I see no hope for a cure. Sometimes I say to myself that I don't know anyone on the current team, their names in the box score could be those of the Harvard junior varsity, but when I pick up the newspaper during the season and turn to the sports page, the day always seems to go a little better when I discover that they have won.

All of this started when *Sports Illustrated* for whom I had written my participatory adventures (football with the Detroit Lions, boxing the light heavyweight champion—Archie Moore, pitching in a postseason All-Star Game) arranged for me to join the Celtics for preseason practice and in the hopes I could be inserted in an exhibition game in order to write about the experience.

It was not a comfortable assignment. As a basketball player I am hopelessly handicapped. Though built along the proper lines (6-feet-4 and 180 pounds), I had hardly ever played the game—a deprived youth. To begin with, I have very uncertain feelings about the basketball itself, perhaps because I can't pick it up without using two hands. I know that's difficult for anyone, but I feel comfortable with a ball I can get my fingers around, a baseball, a tennis ball, even a football. To me, laying hands on a basketball is like patting a heifer's flank.

I had need of a tutor. I found a good one. A few weeks before I was due in Boston, Bill Bradley, the Knicks' star forward at the time, took me in hand for some coaching. We had some one-on-one practices in the Downtown Athletic Club gymnasium—an interesting venue because a strong summer breeze whistling in through windows high in the walls required a lot of windage for Bradley's long set shots to settle into the basket. He spent some time with me. He set out some chairs in a long staggered row and suggested I spend hours dribbling a basketball down their length. On defense he advised me to watch the belly button of the player opposite me. "That is when he has the ball," he said. "You can't be faked out if you watch the guy's belly button. The only player with a belly button that sashays around is Oscar Robertson's."

Bradley had an interesting notion for dunking—an art, incidentally, about six inches away from my ever achieving. It was that inner-city kids had a special affinity for dunking because many had grown up on city playgrounds with baskets with no nets, so that the only tactile evidence of their skill was to touch the rim. For other kids playing in gymnasiums their subconscious satisfaction was from hearing the sweet sound of the basketball going through the mesh of the strings—*swish* as some sportscasters put it in their play-by-play commentaries.

So armed with this important information—the stuff about the belly buttons and so forth—I left for Boston and checked into the Lenox Hotel. The schedule called for us to leave the hotel and arrive midmorning at a gym that overlooked Massachusetts Avenue. Nothing fancy at all. A bit rundown, like the hotel. No lockers set aside for us. We carried our practice stuff over in our kit bags. We dressed and went up one flight to the gym floor. Banks of seats along one side. Big bay windows looking out on the avenue. Not a smart dresser among any of us. I don't remember that anything the veterans were wearing suggested that they were Celtics. We looked like refugees from a rag-pickers convention. The equipment manager hadn't arrived. No basketballs. One of the rookies began running very swift laps, to make an impression, I suppose. No sign of Bill Russell, the player-coach, however, who would have been the one to impress. So we stood around.

Finally, *thunk, thunk,* and an ancient basketball that someone had found in a dressing room locker turned up on the floor. The rookies stood around nervously, not sure they should enter the kind of low-key playground scrimmaging the veterans had initiated. I stood very much apart from all this, vaguely wondering how to keep my notes. With the Detroit Lions I kept a notebook in my helmet, into which I wrote from time to time. No way to secrete a notebook on the person of a basketball player! I put my notebook on one of the seats, intending to drift over to it to jot down the more important observations.

Bill Russell arrived 30 minutes late, and along with him a bagful of basketballs. The Great Bearded One, as my teammates referred to him. He seemed immensely bored by the practice sessions. He didn't dress for play himself—slimly cut street clothes to fit his long shanks; he had a whistle as I recall, on a cord. To my surprise his drills included some amazingly basic exercises, as if he really couldn't think of anything else to do—how to throw a basketball for distance, for example, with an outward flip of the wrist at the end of the toss so the ball doesn't curve in flight. So it was odd to watch Sam Jones, say, who has been throwing basketballs the length of the court for dozens of years, stepping up to the line to do it yet once again as if a pupil at a summer basketball camp.

We ran laps, many, many of them—easy enough for Russell to call when he couldn't think of anything else for us. Our sneakers thundered on the wooden floor like a stampede. In the August heat they were exhausting. I remember one of the rookies, a Princeton graduate, leaning out the gym window and vomiting into Massachusetts Avenue—a surprising sight from below, I would have thought . . . a face suddenly appearing at a window, etc.

I think it was the first day when Russell explained the plays. There were only six basic plays. Each one had variations—backdoors, reverses and so on, and while I wrote them down in my seatside notebook, and saw them in my mind's eye as I lay sleepless in my stark hotel room, they vanished utterly on the few occasions that Russell sent me out on the floor in scrimmages. I would see John Havlicek hold up two fingers as he came down the floor and then something would happen that wasn't in any of my clumsy diagrams. What I did then was to start a kind of evasive action, mindlessly running helter-skelter through the pack, trying to "get open," hoping in the process to set up involuntary picks and cause chaos in the opposition. My teammates took very little notice of this. They went about their business rather calmly and they would score.

On the few occasions I was thrown the ball in a scrimmage, my practice was to bounce it once and then stand immobile, even if no defender was anywhere near me, and look around for someone to throw it to, often from deep in the backcourt. The guards, Sam Jones or John Havlicek, wearing half-grins, would come back across the center line and bail me out.

Defense was easier, at least in theory . . . simply a matter of finding my opposite and sticking with him, trying to front him, keeping myself between him and the basket. I was never quite sure what "boxing out" was, but I did some pushing when I thought it was appropriate. I did a lot of staring at bellies.

I rode the pines, as they say, through a week or so of the exhibition season. Finally, Bill Russell put me in a game against the Atlanta Hawks. He did this in the fourth quarter when the Celtics were hopelessly out of the game. I knelt at the scoring table and reported, vaguely surprised that someone sitting there didn't say, "What??"

I don't remember much about the game itself. I recall a certain amount of feckless charging about, usually with my back to the ball in the hope that no one would throw it to me. I felt much more confident on defense, where ball-handling was not a requirement.

Within a minute or so, however, I hacked an Atlanta player under the basket. I heard the referee say, after he'd blown his whistle, "You can't do that, you know," rather kindly, as if telling me something I really should have known. I stood mournfully at the foul line watching the Hawk sink his two free throws.

I finally did get the ball on offense. I must have turned at an inappropriate moment and stared at someone who whipped it to me, *whap*, and there I was. Did the image of a "hot potato" come to mind? I can't say that it did, but I do recall that the Hawk guarding me was not looking at my belly, but straight into my eyes! Had my posture on the court suggested that I couldn't make a smart move on him? Whatever, I noticed a teammate, Rich Johnson, maneuvering about behind the Hawk defender, his arms aloft . . . and I flipped the ball to him, two-handed of course, and he turned and popped in a little hook.

So in the box score I got an A for an assist and an F for the hacking foul—just the marks, it occurred to me, that turned up on my school report cards for English and math respectively.

When asked by friends curious about my basketball adventure I often describe that game. Sometimes I tell the more gullible, especially of the female variety, what Mark Twain's Huck Finn calls a "stretcher"—that Bill Russell, seeing that the game was out of hand, had sent me in to substitute for John Havlicek, and that my teammates on the floor raised the level of their game to make up for my deficiencies as a point guard. Slowly our group began to gain—the Hawks worried by this new presence on the floor, an unknown factor, perhaps the owner of a devastating long-range two-handed set shot.

1966 NBA World Championship wristwatch

In fact, all I did—so I tell my audience—was run up and down the sidelines yelling in encouragement . . . a kind of mobile cheerleader. Finally, with a minute or so left in the game the Celtics had hauled themselves up to within striking distance, and Russell felt that he had a chance of winning, or at least tying. So he took me out and put Havlicek back in. The Celtics lost. The most stretched part of my "stretcher" was that I'd gone over to Russ in the locker room afterwards and told him that by taking me out he'd made a bad tactical error! Imagine having the nerve to do *that!*

In any case, the team recovered from the Atlanta loss and went on to win the championship that year, a bitter-sweet triumph in a sense, because it marked the end of the playing careers of both Bill Russell and Sam Jones.

I went out to Los Angeles to watch the seventh and final game of the championship series. High in the rafters of the Forum hung a great cluster of balloons. They were to be let loose and float to the floor in celebration of the expected Laker victory. Their team with Wilt Chamberlain, Elgin Baylor, Jerry West, and company were heavily favored to win. A very tense situation yet I remember minutes before gametime Satch Sanders reading a copy of *Yachting* in his cubicle.

The game was close. The clinching basket was a set shot of Don Nelson's that hit the back rim, bounced several feet straight up, and then dropped down into the net. The only disappointed Celtic was Bill Russell whose *mano a mano* duel with Chamberlain was truncated when the Lakers' great center left the game midway through the final period . . . it spoiled the nicety of their rivalry being played out to the end.

I sat next to Red Auerbach in the stands. When Nelson's shot dropped in, he leaned back and lit his victory cigar—that famous signature gesture of his. He took a puff or two. Just then, a Lakers fan, her face contorted with the agony of watching her team go down to defeat—I got a good look at her—raised an aerosol can of shaving cream and doused the cigar with a quick glob of white foam. It was the only time I ever saw Auerbach slightly flustered.

I'm told he doesn't light up any more in the FleetCenter where smoking is prohibited. After the game, he lights up in a restaurant with the mysterious and far-fetched name of Legal Seafoods, where the menu reads "no smoking in the dining room except for Red Auerbach."

The team celebrated that night. Larry Siegfried had such a night of it that the next morning he had to be supported to the airplane in a wheelchair. I happened to be standing at the end of the ramp when he was wheeled, near comatose, head lolling, into the plane. Three nuns were standing close by. "Look at that poor child," one of them said. I leaned in and said, "He is a member of the team that won the championship last night." She shook her head. "What a brutal game it must have been," she said.

Not long after, the Celtics gave me a championship watch. When he handed it to me, John Havlicek joked that the team never could have done it without me. I wear the watch to this day—an Omega with little brown basketballs for the numbers, a green shamrock leaf at the center under which are the words, "World Champion Boston Celtics." On airplanes I look at my watch a lot so that maybe my seat partner will catch sight of it ("Hey, I can't help noticing that watch of yours"). Actually, what I wear on my wrist is not the original watch. At some point in the seventies, driving along the Massachusetts Turnpike in a heavy snowstorm, I reached out the window to brush away the snow from the windshield and somehow, caught up in the wipers, the wrist band snapped and the watch flew off. I saw it go. I pulled over, stopped the car then backed up. With my wife at the wheel and driving slowly along the Turnpike shoulder, I scrambled around in the beam from the headlights, wary of the oncoming traffic, and finally spotted it. It had been squashed flat.

Mal Graham and George Plimpton take the ball up the court during an exhibition game. This archival photo is from the private collection of George Plimpton.

I kept the watch and was thinking of making a paperweight or something of the sort with it. In the meantime, without my knowledge, my wife had spoken with someone at the Celtics and told of them of my loss, my moan of despair, and not long after *another* watch, identical to the one squashed flat, arrived, and I wear it to this day. I rarely take it off. It has broken down a couple of times but I have had it fixed. I intend to wear it as long as my own internal machinery continues to function. Of course, if I were to have lunch with Bill Russell, that's another matter. I think I'd leave it at home. I'm not sure he would understand. ♣

BLEEDING GREEN

"The Celtics aren't a team, they're a way of life."

RED AUERBACH

CELTICS
PRIDE

"If you never played for the Boston Celtics,
you never really played professional basketball."

LARRY BIRD

"The Celtics aren't a team," Red Auerbach is fond of saying, "they're a way of life."

And More. The *Boston Celtics* are an institution, better known around the world than any other team in *any* sport, a universal symbol of success and excellence. Their name is synonymous with winning. Next to the word success, dictionaries could picture the Celtics logo, the cocky leprechaun jauntily twirling a basketball while leaning on a shillelagh. The Celtics define success.

They are the greatest name in basketball history, the sport's most storied franchise. Celtics *success* is unmatched as, decade after decade, the Green has dominated roundball as no other team in any sport. The Celts have scaled basketball's Everest 16 times during their 50 seasons, a model of prosperity and consistency for a half a century.

They don't have as many championships as hockey's Montreal Canadiens (24 Stanley Cup inscriptions) or baseball's New York Yankees (22 World Series rings). But at little more than half the age, the Celtics have a far superior title ratio while collecting those 16 NBA crowns. And the Celts' eight consecutive championships from 1959 through 1966 easily surpass the five straight won by the 1949-53 Yankees and 1956-60 Canadiens. Nor can any team approach the Celtics' domination of nine championships in 10 years and 11 in 13 seasons.

And these are "world" championships and don't include division pennants. The Celtics have collected 24 of those while suffering only six losing seasons since the 1950 arrival of Red Auerbach, the brash architect who transformed a sad sack doormat to champion while establishing a tradition for winning.

Winning is what the Celtics are all about, the legacy passed like a torch from one Green generation to the next with extraordinary continuity. The result is a consistency that has known few and brief valleys along with all the peaks as the team has earned at least two NBA crowns in each decade from the fifties through the eighties.

And it's not only the frequency of Celtics triumph that's remarkable but *how* they've done it, as the Horatio Alger of professional sports teams. It's an unlikely story of basketball's ugly and puny duckling, unwanted, underfunded, undertalented and only half-jokingly called the Smeltics transformed into a swan envied as hoopdom's showcase franchise.

It is the stuff of which legends are made. And *mystiques*. "Other teams have histories," Bob Ryan has written. "The Celtics have a mystique."

The Celtics mystique isn't easily defined. Nor is Celtics pride.

"I don't know if those are the right words, but there certainly has been something special," Don Nelson once said of the intangible he has long experienced from both sides of the court, both as a celebrated Celtic and an opposing coach.

"I've given it a lot of thought and suppose a lot of things factor into it. Mostly, though, it's Auerbach. Red made this mystic thing."

"When everyone tries to think about what the Celtics mystique is," Bob Cousy has said, "we should just point to Arnold. He personifies what Celtics mystique means."

Of course. Arnold "Red" Auerbach. He arrived in Boston four and a half decades ago as a brash 32-year-old basketball genius and invented the Celtics way. While assembling a dynamic Green Machine that won year after year, he created a franchise for the ages.

Like a roundball Arthur Fiedler, Auerbach is the maestro who has orchestrated it all, the glue that has connected era after era after era of Celtics winning, first as coach, then as general manager, president, the guru who has presided over it all. He's the bedrock of a franchise that carries his indelible stamp. And even though he "retired" nearly a dozen years ago when he handed over the day-to-day reigns to Jan Volk, he is still a presence as the Celtics' patriarch, their Godfather, basketball's Mr. Chips as the only survivor of the league's birth still on the scene.

"Auerbach is the lion of winter, sharp as ever, still Red after all these years," sportswriter Dan Shaughnessy has written, deftly describing Red as the Celtics' "legend-in-residence."

Red Auerbach: wily, headstrong, combustible—a master communicator, motivator, psychologist, and schemer. A visionary. And a dictator.

"A benevolent dictator, but a dictator all the same," he'd say while directing Celtics championships each of his last eight seasons as coach (so much for "three-peat"), while establishing both himself and his team as legends. "There is room for only one boss, and that's me."

Before there can be cliches like *mystique* and *pride* there has to be *winning,* and Auerbach taught the Celtics how and made them winners. He was dedicated to it, driven by it, and it became contagious.

"Winning is what it's all about, what makes this fun," he told his troops. "There's no substitution for winning, none. Never forget that."

"Red cannot stand the thought of losing," Bill Russell wrote long ago. "Anyone who has ever come to the Celtics was immediately instilled with this philosophy. If you don't play to win, Auerbach has no place for you."

"I found players who wanted to win," explained Auerbach, who assembled his jigsaw puzzle piece by piece, carefully handpicking not only talented players earmarked for a role, but smart ones, adjustable ones, players with character and an appetite for winning. "They didn't have 'Celtics pride' or tradition when they got here. They acquired it. It rubbed off on them."

The year was 1946. Walter Brown had just bought an NBA franchise. Then came choosing a nickname. He and aide Howie McHugh kicked around ideas—Unicorns, Whirlwinds, Olympics. None worked. Then it came to Brown: "Wait, I've got it—the Celtics. We'll call them the Celtics . . . Boston Celtics. The name has a great basketball tradition . . . and Boston is full of Irishmen. Yes, that's it. We'll put them in green uniforms and call them the Boston Celtics."

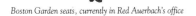

Boston Garden seats, currently in Red Auerbach's office

THE SPIRIT OF THE CELTICS

The Celtics were his team. He was the rock they were built upon, a hockey man who mortgaged his home and risked his savings to keep alive what would become basketball's most successful team. His name was Walter Brown, and the symbolic number 1 is retired in his memory.

"If it wasn't for Walter," Red Auerbach says, "there wouldn't be the Boston Celtics." Auerbach knows better than anyone. Red was in the trenches with Brown during those shaky years in the early fifties when the franchise teetered on the brink of bankruptcy as Boston took scant interest in the Celts. It was a hockey town, and, as Boston Bruins President, Walter should realize that, friends said. The situation was hopeless, he was told, and many, including his wife Marjorie, urged Brown to give up his basketball dream before he woke up in the poorhouse.

A decade later, when Walter died at age 59 in 1964 after seeing his Celtics win seven NBA championships to be celebrated around the world, it was Auerbach who retired *numero uno* for the man who started it all.

"Walter Brown was

WALTER BROWN

one of the greatest men who ever lived," Auerbach says. "He was a magnificent human being who personified everything good in sports, a pure sportsman who cared about people and was totally unselfish. Over the years I always tried to live up to everything Walter stood for because I admired him so much. He was so unique, totally honest and totally fair, the nicest man I've ever known. I loved him. So did all our players. We all truly did. The Celtics family thing started with him."

"And when you began talking about the great Celtic tradition," Bob Cousy says, "that's where it started, with Walter Brown."

One of a kind, Walter also was human. His temper occasionally matched his Irish charm. He'd blow off steam at the league commissioner or a referee, even at some of his stars . . . and usually apologize the next day. And Walter could be headstrong, although it was that stubbornness that saved the franchise for Boston as he disregarded advice and stuck with the Celtics.

Mostly, though, Walter was warm and outgoing and generous, although as a sportsman without deep pockets he couldn't always afford to be. Never the big shot, he was down to earth and without pretenses. His Garden door was always open, to players and the bull gang, reporters and concession hawkers . . . even to fans wandering in off Causeway Street. Walter was totally accessible—to a fault, Auerbach felt sometimes. Red became irritated when unable to get his boss alone, perhaps to talk contract. So he'd steer Walter down the hall to the men's room, and salary would be agreed on in the time it took to wash their hands.

"There never was need for a written contract," Red says of dealing with the man enshrined in both the basketball and hockey halls of fame. "Walter's word was sufficient. Hell, we didn't even need to shake hands."

The NBA required contracts for players, though, so Frank Ramsey would simply sign a blank one and let Walter fill in the figures. "If the world was filled with Walter Browns," Ramsey says, "there'd be no need for lawyers."

Negotiations with Bill Russell, basketball's highest-paid player under Walter , took longer. "Walter would ask me how much I wanted and I'd tell him," Russell says. "He'd hand me a pen and say, 'Sign it.'"

"Walter had a nobility and was a very decent human being. The true secret of Celtics success stems from his spirit."

"We've never allowed Walter's spirit to die in the Celtics organization and never will," Auerbach says. "He'll always be number one."

PLAYING FOR THE CELTICS

I remember that first training camp after the team was formed, we stayed in a dormitory inside the Boston Arena a floor below from where we practiced. We all slept in this one big room. We'd run through the downtown streets for conditioning. It was some beginning."

VIRGIL VAUGHN (1946-47)

If I remember, Washington had Red Auerbach as coach back then. We had nothing . . . but a lot of good guys and memorable times."

JOHN SIMMONS (1946-47)

As soon as I arrived in Boston, I sensed it was different from the other teams I played for. Their only concern was winning. There was no personal jealousy. The other players wanted me to do well, because if everyone did well . . . the Celtics won. No one cared who scored, they just wanted to score."

BAILEY HOWELL
(1966-70)

Walter Brown was the nicest man I ever knew. When Doggie Julian replaced Honey Russell as coach, I got out. Walter came over and apologized to me, saying he put Doggie in charge and he had to go along with his coach, no matter how much it hurt him."

JACK GARFINKEL (1946-49)

Being drafted in the first round to play for the Celtics was like getting the call. You were chosen. They didn't go after players unless they had a reason. I remember thinking that when they picked me. 'The Celtics want me . . .'

CEDRIC MAXWELL (1977-85)

There was a feeling you got when playing with the Celtics. It was a sense that this was different from anything else you would do in basketball. The goal was to bring another championship to its rightful home."

JERRY SICHTING (1985-87)

Great players, not great egos. There was a common goal. To play the best basketball possible ever…all the time. Play the best basketball and winning would happen. There was never pressure on winning and losing, just playing your absolute best."

BILL WALTON (1985-87)

There's more to being a Celtic than winning. There are standards for who you are, on and off the court. The guidelines were established long ago by great players and fine men. To be a Celtic, you had to live up to all the traditions."

CHRIS FORD (1978-82)

Auerbach knew what it took to win, and the formula was simple: teamwork. He preached it. He demanded it. It became the Celtics' hallmark. Red loathed individual play, one-man shows. Basketball was a team game. Move the ball, run—hit the open man. It was also a game to be played on both ends of the floor, and he put a new emphasis on defense, largely unappreciated before, so largely ignored.

Auerbach convinced his stars to sacrifice for the common good, to subordinate self for the team. He unified ego, harnessing it in the same direction for a common cause: winning. He kept his collection of stars, some of the greatest who ever played, focused on the team instead of the individual. Only one statistic mattered: victories.

Significantly, no Celtic has ever led the league in scoring, few are even among the annual leaders. Yet no team approaches the crowd of Celtics in the Hall of Fame. (Incredibly, seven players of the 1960–61 squad alone are enshrined at Springfield, and that's not counting Auerbach or Walter Brown.)

Reminding them that it was a privilege to be a Celtic, Red made his players believers in his team ethic, convinced by all the championship rings and money shares, and underscored as they helped hoist a new banner to the rafters most every year. And season in, season out Auerbach motivated them, never letting them become content, making them hunger for more success.

Not only did the system produce championships, but it heightened another element of the Celtics tradition: family. As Russell has said, "There were key people, Red Auerbach, Bob Cousy, Bill Russell, John Havlicek, but there were no stars. We were in this to accomplish things together, and we really looked out for each other. I have great affection for many of my Celtics teammates, great affection. I guess love is the proper word."

"When you talk about the Celtic tradition, it is more than a matter of winning," Auerbach once told Joe Fitzgerald. "We just didn't play the best. We also wanted to look the best, dress the best, act the best. It was a certain championship feeling."

And all that is the legacy that's been passed along from Celtics generation to generation as success has bred success to build the Celtics legend.

While Auerbach is at the heart of the mystique that revolves around him, there's a lot more to it—a mix of people and places, sights and sounds.

There's that Horatio Alger thing, of course—the Celtics' improbable beginnings and struggle for survival. It was Walter Brown who laid the cornerstone as head of the Garden-Arena Corporation. When he founded the team 50 years ago, it was a stepchild on the Boston sports scene, born in a city that was a hockey hotbed during the wintertime and considered basketball a game for giraffes running around in their underwear.

Although invented only 100 miles away in Springfield, basketball had never caught on in Boston—or generally around New England, although there were a few pockets of interest, like those supporting college powerhouses at Holy Cross and the University of Rhode Island. Dr. James Naismith's invention had become a city game popular on the dusty playgrounds and cramped gyms of New York, Philadelphia and Chicago. Not so in Boston, where most public high schools didn't even play roundball.

So, unlike hockey, basketball had no roots in Boston—and thus there was little interest in the game. And it didn't help that this new team was trying to make it in a new league also without history and recognizable attractions. Joe Fulks was coming to town? So what—who's Joe Fulks? Max Zaslofsky? Never heard of him.

Walter "Randy" Randall went to work at the Boston Garden when it opened in 1928 and served the Celtics as equipment manager from the day the club was born until his death on May 21, 1985. Calling Randall a faithful employee, however, falls far short of the mark. Like so many in the family, Randy bled Celtics green. For years, Randy's seat was a fixture at the end of the Boston bench. But he never returned to his spot after being ejected from a game by Mendy Rudolph.

THE PARQUET

Rudy "Spider" Edwards

The flooring, in the proccess of being reassembled after a resurfacing.

The antique and venerable parquet is a Celtics relic born of desperation and ingenuity. When the Celts came along in 1946, lumber was scarce, among shortages lingering from World War II. Walter Brown needed wood flooring in a hurry, enough for two basketball courts: one for Boston Garden, another for Boston Arena. Home games for the Celtics would be played in both buildings. And the courts had to be portable, to be easily stored during events. A top Boston floormaker, Tony DiNatale, had some oak scraps, crosscut from a Tennessee forest. Cleverly, he wove the hardwood remnants into a distinctive and durable mosaic that has become an imitated Celtics landmark and part of sports folklore, recognized wherever there is television, and associated with the Celtics and their winning tradition.

Originally, the floor cost $11,000. It has 247 panels, 5-foot squares of 1 1/2 -inch thick planking screwed together. Nearly 1,000 bolts fasten the panels in an alternating pattern.

(Reflecting the parquet's celebrity, the television sitcom *Cheers* once devoted an episode to discovering the number of bolts. At last count it was 988, Carla.)

In the late fifties, when the Celtics ceased playing at the Arena, the parquet was shipped crosstown to the Garden, where sections of both courts were to be interchanged as needed. Over the decades, worn-out pieces of the jigsaw puzzle have been replaced, but some original parts may remain.

The checkerboard was moved from the Garden to the FleetCenter a year ago along with versions of the green-and-white banners, a transition that gave historical Celtics continuity from top to bottom in the new building.

Long ago the parquet became part of Red Auerbach's psychological warfare against paranoid guests . . . opponents who suspected Auerbachian mischief at every crooked turn in the old Garden, blaming anything and everything on Red's obsessive dedication to gaining a Celtics edge. Their complaint wasn't so much that they felt they had to dribble differently there, but that the aged parquet deadened the bounce. It was the dead spots that haunted them like a mine field. The Celtics knew their locations, it was charged, and not only avoided them but steered opponents there.

Those claims delighted Auerbach, first as coach and later as general manager and president. "If teams felt that way, I used it for an advantage by playing with their minds," he says now. "If they felt that floor gave us an edge, I wanted to keep them thinking that way."

So Red rarely responded to the charges. Not a word. He'd just usually smirk and puff thoughtfully on his cigar. The master manipulator didn't have to talk to psyche foes and distract them.

At its 50th birthday, the parquet still sparkles. Resurfaced at least three times (1972, 1993, and 1995) it is buffed lovingly by dapper Rudy "Spider" Edwards, who for decades has been gliding his big mop across the surface as admiring fans cheer him on.

The polished checkerboard glistens in high gloss, mirroring all those banners above, reflecting the 16 NBA championships won on the parquet.

And if it wasn't bad enough that this was a sport that Bostonians didn't care about in a league that nobody knew about, the Celtics were dreadful on the court—the worst (well, tied for last). It was three strikes that nearly spelled out. The Celtics were hardly noticed—ignored except as a joke—and the apathy translated into a large financial drainpipe. And after four years of hemorrhaging, Garden-Arena stockholders quit on the team. That's when Brown stubbornly stepped up and risked all to keep his dream team alive.

It was the wobbliest of starts: undertalented, underfunded, and unappreciated. If Bostonians had been told that just two of the new league's 11 teams would still be doing business in the same town a half century later, they wouldn't have been surprised. Told that one would be New York would be predictable; told the other would be Boston would have been a shocker. No way.

All of this feeds into the Celtics mystique, of course. Everyone loves a great American success story, and this one was a pip. Probably the sports world's best ever: an orphan team saved by a kindly Samaritan, pulling itself up by its sneaker laces to become basketball's greatest team and a household name known around the world.

It took a while, but Boston finally began supporting the team as fans became part of the mystique, too. They began noticing the Celtics upon the arrival of Auerbach, Cousy, and Macauley in 1950, and paid more attention with the coming of the dynasty. The Celts may have been *too* successful, as the town took the success for granted: another spring, another flag. Only twice during that 11-titles-in-13-years reign did Celtics home attendance average 10,000. Basketball's greatest team ever—a colossus that New York or Los Angeles would have built monuments to—couldn't even fill its own building except at playoff time. The Celts were a success everywhere but at their own box office.

Boston didn't fully appreciate the Celtics until the dynasty ended in 1969, when fans realized what was lost. So the second coming of success was more savored. And support mushroomed with the arrival of the third championship era in the eighties. From December 1980 until their final game at the Garden in May 1995, there were no empty seats.

It had taken time, but the Celtics had built one of sports' most loyal and enthusiastic followings. Boston had become a sophisticated basketball town peopled by knowledgeable and passionate fans devoted to the Green Team. The city that had long taken pride in the Celtics now was proving it. Through it all, Celtics fans were special, even when they weren't filling the Garden every game.

"Our fans had a way of lifting us to another level," Jo Jo White has said. "They were extremely knowledgeable and, to say the least, enthusiastic."

One time *too* enthusiastic—during the Celtics' marathon thriller with Phoenix during the 1976 playoffs, attended by 15,319 zealots and one airhead. At the end of the second overtime, apparently carried away by the game's hysteria, an irate fan ran out and threw a punch at referee Richie Powers, who belted back before the customer was carted away—hopefully to another court.

And there was the time fans pummeled Guy Rodgers during a wild 1962 playoff game. The Philadelphia villain had sought sanctuary to escape an enraged Jim Loscutoff, who had chased him around the court with such menace that Rodgers armed himself with a photographer's stool before dashing into the crowd. Bad decision. It required Boston police to rescue him.

Perhaps more typical of Celtics clientele was the fan who starred in another memorable Garden moment—Bob Cousy's emotional farewell on St. Patrick's Day 1963. During a tearful pause in Cousy's halftime speech, an upper-balcony resident

Celtics fans seldom are at a loss for words—written or verbal. Here, the message is clear for the visiting Detroit Pistons. Not all the signs were disparaging in nature. "Bird's Nest," "McHale's Army" and "Hail to the Chief" were also popular. Even the opposition could be toasted. One of the classiest exhibitions by a group of fans anywhere came during game 7 of the Eastern Finals against Philidelphia in 1982. When it became obvious to the Garden faithful that the Sixers would win, the crowd in unison thundered the chant "Beat L. A."

FOLLOWING SPREAD:

The Celtics fans are as much a part of Boston's basketball tradition as the players. Rita Kissane, left, waves a towel, while Joanne Borzakian raises a salute during a midgame tribute to their heroes.

THE VOICE OF THE CELTICS

BY JOE FITZGERALD

Johnny Most was the "Voice of the Celtics," broadcasting games with delivery that endeared him to the Celtics faithful. A relief of Most hangs in the Basketball Hall of Fame in recognition of his unique contribution to the sport. Most was as much a Celtic as the players wearing the green-and-white. "Nonpartisan" was not a title he sought. With affection, Tom Heinsohn once said of Most: "Johnny's broadcasts have led some people to think the Celtics played a doubleheader—one game they saw and the game Most announced." Most broadcast Celtics games for 37 seasons starting in 1953. He died in 1993, at age 69.

It was near the end of his life, well beyond the end of his career, and Johnny Most sat in a Boston hospital room, five days after the amputation of both legs, searching for words that might convey the overwhelming gratitude within him.

Hundreds of cards lined the walls of his room, with many more arriving daily, as the phone kept ringing and friends like Larry Bird kept stopping by. And there he was in the middle of it all—a man who made his living with words—trying so hard to say thanks.

"To every Celtics fan who's shown me love," he said, "I just want to say that sometimes love gets shunted aside, and though it may seem to have been unappreciated, it never has been, not for a single moment."

He allowed that thought to hang for a second, then, with a wink, confided, "I figure God's going to coach me out of this."

"By God, you mean Red (Auerbach)?" he was asked, kiddingly.

"Red? No. He's St. Peter."

And with that, the familiar gravelly voice that might have been the most recognizable voice in New England—the voice of the Celtics for 37 seasons from "high above courtside"—filled the room with laughter born of gallows humor.

That was Johnny Most, irrepressible and unpredictable.

Though synonymous with the success of the team he covered, Johnny had great empathy for folks more acquainted with rejection and defeat.

"I'm a homely man," he'd sometimes muse. "I know that. I look in the mirror. I was always the one who made everyone else at the party laugh, then went home alone with a newspaper under my arm. I think that's why I came to love Carl Sandburg's writing, because he had this philosophy which said true beauty lies in a compassion for ugliness. That was always my feeling, too: I have to better myself in other ways because of the kisser I haven't got.

"Love comes in many forms, and one of them is compassion for the downtrodden, for the adverse, for things that don't look good, for things that don't work, or have gone aground. That's what is missing in this world today, real love. I'd like to think I have it."

Then he'd get behind a mike and eviscerate the opposition, vilifying foes—McDirty! McFilthy! McNasty!—and providing Boston listeners with highly emotional accounts of the enemy's sneaky

JOHNNY MOST

tricks and dirty deeds. It was magnificent theater, truly unique, making him as much a part of Celtics lore as the legends whose exploits he dutifully detailed.

He loved to tell of the time one of his favorite foils, Buffalo's Bob Kauffman, yelled to him during pregame warmups, "Hey, Johnny, when do I get to wear the white hat?"

"When you put on the green jersey," Most hollered back, as players from both teams laughed.

"People call, hearing him for the first time, to tell me he's a homer," Red Auerbach often told banquet crowds. "And I tell them, 'You're damn right he is; that's the way we want him.'"

Johnny took issue with the concept of homer, however.

"I don't consider it anything to apologize for because I believe most objectivity is phony. It's nonsense. If you're telling me a man can travel with a team for 25, 30 years and remain completely neutral, well, I'm sorry, but I just don't believe that. The honesty of my broadcasts is that I love the Celtics. OK? I've been with them a long time. I have breakfast and dinner with them. And now someone's telling me I've got to pretend I don't care who wins? No, my philosophy is this: be yourself, be real."

And that's what he was, inimitably so.

"Every broadcast is the only broadcast, know what I mean? Tonight's game is the only one that ever existed, meaning I have to pull everything out of my bag of tricks. Each game is a separate drama, a whole new set of emotions. If I bring pleasure to people, if I make them laugh a little, give them a couple hours of enjoyment, then I've done my job. Basically, I'm an entertainer, and I have to believe people really want to listen to me.

It is egotistical, yes, but if you don't feel that way, you can't go on. I want to believe people listening to me are really enjoying themselves."

In Boston, that was easy to believe.

On the road, however, where eavesdroppers took offense to Johnny's well-known partisanship, tempers often flared.

In St. Louis, he ended up on the floor wrestling Hawks owner Ben Kerner. In Philadelphia, he told his color man to take over and then waded into the hostile crowd in pursuit of a foul-mouthed critic. In Syracuse, in San Antonio, in New York, in Los Angeles, old-timers still tell stories of the nights Johnny Most was there.

As referee Sid Borgia once noted, "Auerbach and Most could start a riot at a high mass."

Johnny's popularity was so great that sound-alike contests were common all over New England, often with Johnny himself brought in as a judge, sharing personal tips with the contestants: "Try gargling with Drain-O every night."

He was a character.

But he was also a gifted poet, and a World War II airman who flew 28 combat missions as a gunner on a B-24, earning seven battle stars.

Cigarettes and coffee and all-night bull sessions in lounges all over the league were part of his legend, as Kevin McHale joked the night a black-tie dinner was held in Johnny's honor, two years before his death.

"When God pulled Lazarus out of

a grave, he had nothing on Johnny; Johnny's been doing that for years. If he had been on the *Titanic* when it went down, two days later you'd have seen him doing a backstroke in the North Atlantic saying, 'Hey, salt water's not bad once you get used to it.'

"Coming from Minnesota, I'd never seen anyone like Johnny. Coming from anywhere, you would never have seen anyone like Johnny. You fans who brought your children here are brave; Johnny Most stories are not for the timid. Everyone used to tell him, 'Johnny, don't smoke on the bus.' Then we all saw how indestructible he is. Now everyone smokes on the bus, and drinks lots of coffee, too. . . ."

But like so many others at the head table that night, McHale wound up putting his heart on his sleeve.

"Seriously, John, you've been the glue that's held us together all these years. He would tell guys like me about guys like Tommy (Heinsohn), so that when we finally met it was as if we already knew them. He brought us all together, and I think a lot of the family tradition and winning we've shared stems from the fact we all felt part of the same thing; we were all Celtics.

"Johnny, we miss you at the games. It's just not the same without you. And despite all I've said tonight, you know how much I love you. We all do."

As illness and ailments took their toll—emphysema, stroke, heart surgery—Most began hearing not just from adoring fans in Boston, but from what might have been seen as a most unlikely group of well-

wishers: Celtics opponents. Warm wishes began pouring in from the likes of Billy Cunningham, Pat Riley, Bill Laimbeer, Walt Frazier, Wes Unseld, Lenny Wilkens, Johnny Kerr, and Jerry West. The list was long and touched him deeply.

"How lucky I am," he said that day in his hospital bed, his amputations notwithstanding. "Lou Gehrig was my hero, growing up in Brooklyn, and I remember the day he called himself the luckiest man on the face of the earth. I guess that's how I feel, too.

"All those years I spent doing games were never for the purpose of anything like this. I just loved what I was doing and believed in what the Celtics represented.

"Now, to think that maybe I've actually added something to the Boston sports scene that won't be duplicated or forgotten . . ."

"No, John," he was told, "there are no maybes about that."

None whatsoever.

Johnny is seen broadcasting from high above courtside (above). His retired microphone, as it appeared in Boston Garden (below), now hangs in his memory in the FleetCenter.

relieved an awkward silence by hollering the instantly classic "We love ya, Cooz!"—ensuring himself a place in Celt folklore.

The Garden itself contributed to the Celtics mystique too, of course.

Some called it the Land of Legends; Auerbach called it a "dump," although not without some affection. The Garden may have been crumbling but gave the Celts a home-court advantage like no other. It was a special Celtics place from top to bottom—from the ancient parquet to the bannered ceiling that symbolized all the championships and honored those who had made them possible. They stretched wall to wall, row after row—like so many sheets strung out on tenement clotheslines, it's been written.

It was a shrine that had a majesty to it despite the outdated building. It was almost mystical, and often psyched out opponents, who strolled in, looked up and down, gulped, and all but conceded. They expected to lose, and usually did—including 48 straight times during an incredible 72-of-73 stretch. And afterward, groping for excuses, losers would blame everything on the building.

Howie McHugh, the Celtics' fiery and fiercely loyal public relations man, was a fixture at Boston Garden until his death in 1983. McHugh was there with founder Walter Brown when the Celtics were born and named. While it was McHugh's job to inform the public about the Celtics, he also offered his thoughts to referees, opinions that once got him bounced from a game.

More likely it was the procession of gifted Celtics parading down the parquet that not only spelled victory, but created the franchise's image of success and the mystique that goes with it.

It was The Cooz igniting another fastbreak . . . Easy Ed arcing a picture hookshot . . . Russell soaring to block a shot or vacuum a rebound . . . Sharman, Sam, and Jo Jo draining sweet jumpers . . . Ramsey and Walton rushing off the bench to the rescue . . . Heinsohn lining a running hook . . . Loscy decking an opponent—accidentally, of course . . . Havlicek running and never stopping . . . K.C., Satch, and DJ hounding opponents, then stealing the ball . . . Cowens and Siggy diving for loose balls . . . Nellie upfaking another patsy . . . Parish and Silas banging the boards . . . Max sweeping a hook, McHale hitting a fallaway . . . Tiny and Reggie pushing the ball upcourt . . . Henderson intercepting a pass . . . Ainge connecting long distance . . . and Bird, well, being Bird.

And through it all, there's M. L. swinging his towel overhead, whipping up the crowd.

It's a former coach named Auerbach sitting in his box, still hectoring referees. And it's Celtic alumni sitting among the fans who used to cheer them—and sometimes vaulting from their seats and onto the court to act as peacemakers.

It's public-address announcers introducing popular heroes.

And from high above courtside, there's gravel-voiced Johnny Most rasping his play-by-play.

And of course, there's Walter Brown. Brown is a huge part of the Celtics mystique, too—not only as the founding father who kept the team alive during difficult times, but for creating the Celtics' sense of family. That started with Walter, who cared about people—especially *his* team. The Celtics tradition is all this and a lot more—like all the team's firsts. And none was more important or left more of an imprint on history than breaking the color line. The Celts were the first NBA team to draft a Black player, the first to start five Blacks, and the first team in any sport to hire a Black coach.

And on and on—the tradition continues, at age 50 a celebration of unparalleled success.

Now the Celtics are busily retooling for another renewal. A fourth coming. Their past has included a few other valleys among all the peaks. Historically, those transitions haven't taken long. A Celtics renaissance soon followed. Of course, Red Auerbach nods matter-of-factly. And the legend will continue, he assures between puffs on his cigar.

"The Celtics," he explains, "are the Celtics." ☘

The friendliest of adversaries, Magic Johnson and Larry Bird cavort during the 1993 ceremonies celebrating Bird's retirement. "Everyone knows what I think about Larry," said Magic. "He's the smartest player in the league. That's where he always excelled . . . Combining talent and intelligence."

Throughout the '80s, the words "Bird" and "Magic" were synonymous with NBA basketball. Every meeting promised a classic confrontation.

PRESERVING CELTICS HISTORY

What are memories without memorabilia?

Over 50 seasons, the Boston Celtics have generated huge portions of both.

Because the Celtics shared Boston Garden with the Bruins, the basketball team shared space in the program with the the hockey team.

As the Celtics grew, so did their publications.

Early media guides were actually called "yearbooks," produced with a dual purpose—to provide information on the team and its players to fans as well as to newspaper writers and broadcasters. As the Celtics began winning championships, the media guides developed into a living history that became as popular with

historians and souvenir collectors as the media.

Over the years, the media guide has expanded and grown into a detailed book approaching 300 pages. Most treasured are those that follow championship seasons—their distinctive covers commemorating another title.

Among the most coveted pieces of Celtics memorabilia is a rare copy of the program from Bob Cousy Day—March 17, 1963.

Cousy was one of the first members of the official Celtics family to recognize the importance of protecting and preserving the Celtics history as it unfolded in programs, media guides, souvenirs, and trophies.

He led an effort that produced a comprehensive display at the New England Sports Museum, which was founded by Dave Cowens. Red Auerbach and John Havlicek have also been key figures in the preservation of Celtics memorabilia.

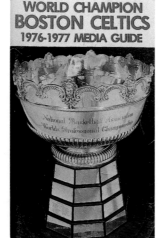

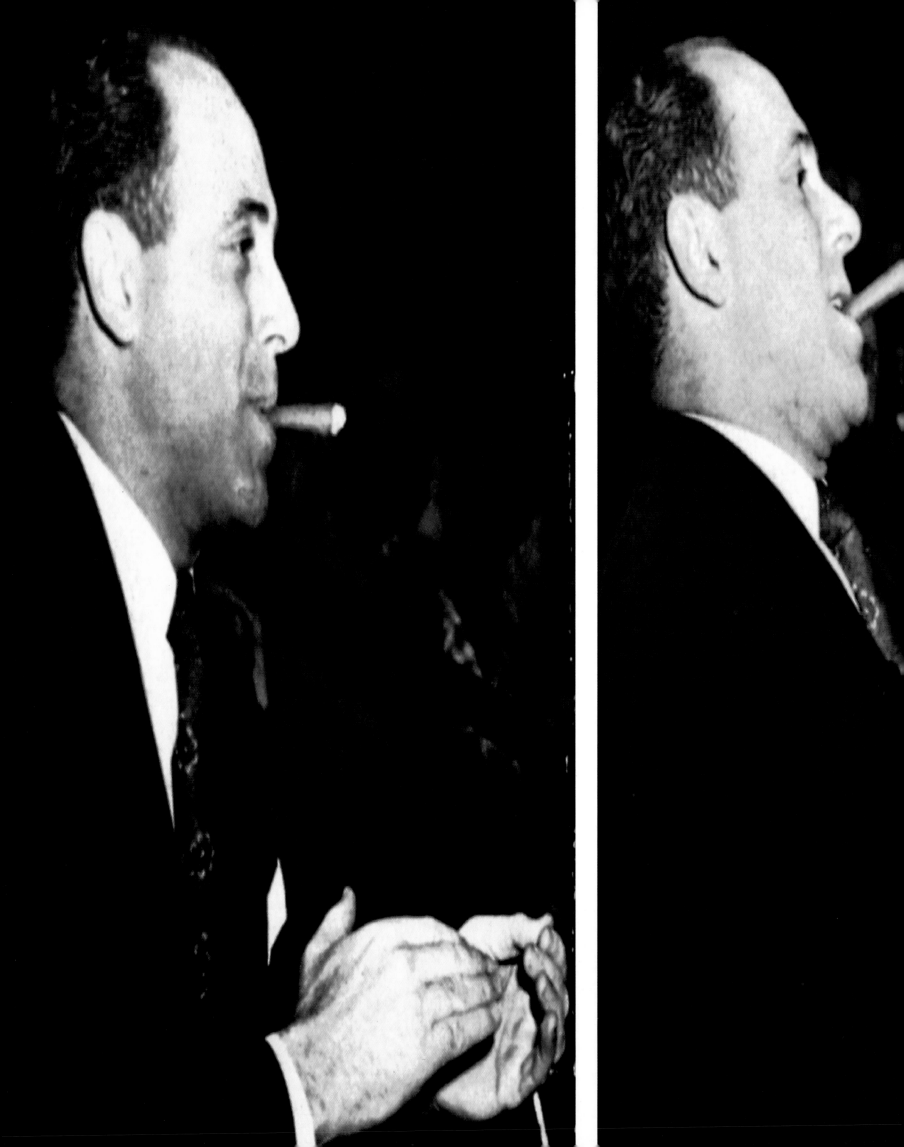

"RED"

" . . . the Celtics' special ingredient."

LARRY BIRD

A
CELTICS
LEGEND

BY JOE FITZGERALD

". . . In sports there can be no democracy . . ."

RED AUERBACH

Bill Russell, whose independent nature was the stuff of legend, was once asked how he coexisted so successfully with Red Auerbach, whose consummate authority was the essence of Boston Celtics basketball.

"What Red and I shared," he replied, "was the most essential ingredient in any relationship: mutual respect. Was I submissive? I'm not sure that's the word I'd use. In order to lead you must know how to follow. Why would I challenge Auerbach? In my mind he was the best coach in the history of professional sports. Period."

Russell's assessment is shared by opponents and supported by records, yet anyone looking for highfalutin sophistication would find barren ground in Auerbach, who believed, most of all, in the simplicity of the game.

"Gentlemen," he told the first team he coached, St. Alban's Prep in Washington, DC, "this thing I hold in my hand is a basketball. The object of this game is to take this ball and stick it into that hole over there. And after it goes through that hole, you've got to all work together as a team to stop the other side from putting it through the hole at the other end. Any questions so far?"

Years later, long after his Celtics had become perennial champions, he delighted in reviving that routine for their edification.

"So many coaches have a tendency to overcoach," John Havlicek noted. "But Red made basketball simple. For instance, blocking out. Some coaches get all caught up in describing the moves of the legs, the reverse pivots, the crossovers, all kinds of stuff like that. Red would just say, '*Stick your forearm into his chest, get your ass against him and don't let him touch the ball!*' See what I mean? He'd explain what he wanted in simple terms, then he'd expect you to go out and do it."

Discipline, the hallmark of Auerbach's coaching, was also reduced to its simplest form.

"It's just a proper response to authority," he contended. "And you can have it without a thousand rules. You get it through respect. I live in a democracy and I believe in democracy, but in sports there can be no democracy, because there simply isn't time for one. So my word was law. The one word I never wanted to hear was *Why?"*

"We could talk to Red," Frank Ramsey remembered. "He'd listen to our suggestions. He wanted his players to contribute ideas. But once he started to talk, that was it. He was the boss and the only response he expected was obedience. If you want to know one of the real secrets to our success, it was this: we all had a respect for authority, and every one of us recognized Red as that authority."

Sid Borgia, a prominent referee of the fifties, marveled over that authority from a distance. "I watched every NBA team, night after night, and got to know how each one operated. I'd see teams go to their huddles and everyone would talk at once, or the coach would talk and no one would listen, or some would listen while others went looking for cups of water. But when Boston went into its huddle only one man talked and everyone else listened, and that man was the Redhead. During those years they kept winning championships Red was surrounded by some of the greatest stars this game has ever known, and when you hold the greats of the game in the palm of your hand, then you are truly master of the ship. It's one thing to have the horses and another thing to know how to ride them, and, boy, did Red ride them well."

Auerbach's concepts were shaped before the league was born, back in World War II when, as a navy lieutenant, he served with Yankee shortstop Phil Rizzuto at the naval base in Norfolk, Virginia.

"Phil told me how (manager) Joe McCarthy was vitally concerned about the image of the Yankees, how he believed the way a team conducted itself off the field had a lot to do with the way it performed on the field. He said Joe would pull aside kids from farms and ghettos and teach them how to tip properly in restaurants, dress properly in public, act properly in places like hotel lobbies, and that fascinated me. A guy like DiMaggio really did look and act like a champion, so it only made sense that if you could get an entire team to look and act the way DiMaggio did, you'd have a hell of a team. I remember thinking that if I ever got to the professional coaching level, I wanted my clubs to look and act like champions, too."

So Auerbach made it a point to draft what he called "my kind of kid."

ARNOLD "RED" AUERBACH

"I've always believed the quality of the person is every bit as important as the quality of the athlete. I wanted a kid who had the ability to absorb coaching, who'd react to whatever I told him, a nice kid on and off

The Boston Celtics had suffered four losing seasons when Arnold "Red" Auerbach became the struggling organization's third head coach in 1950. His arrival was afforded only seven paragraphs in one Boston newspaper. Said owner Walter Brown upon introducing Auerbach, "How long he holds the job depends on what he makes of the sport during the coming season."

The rest is history. Auerbach coached the Celtics to nine NBA championships, including an incredible run of eight straight from 1959–66. His Celtics clubs won 67 percent of their regular-season games (795-397) and 61 percent of their playoff outings (90-58). After leaving coaching following the 1965–66 season, Auerbach directed seven more championship campaigns as general manager and later as president.

the court, not someone who'd be bitching all the time. Some kids become real pains once they get a taste of stardom. Most of all, I wanted a kid who wanted to win so bad he wouldn't think twice about giving me everything he had."

Once he got them, he sold them on a point of view which held that the ultimate victory belonged to the team, not to any of its individually celebrated members.

"Our pride was never rooted in statistics," he explained. "Our pride was in our identity as the Boston Celtics because being a Celtic meant being the best."

Yet that mind-set had to involve the subordination of many egos, and therein lay Auerbach's genius.

The morning after the Celtics won their eighth championship with a 129-96 rout of the Los Angeles Lakers in 1965, Auerbach enjoyed the front page of the Boston Record American *and, of course, a cigar.*

"People don't realize how easily those great teams could have fallen apart at the seams," Easy Ed Macauley pointed out. "You had all these super athletes, each with his own personality and temperament; you had a shifting of race as the league went from predominantly white to predominantly black; you had the very active Boston media fawning over a guy like Cooz and generally understating Russell's contributions; you had great players like Ramsey being asked to sit on the bench. Now you take all these factors together and you begin to realize what a marvelous job Red did keeping them all happy. That was the greatness of Auerbach."

Red was sold on the importance of roles and sold his players on them, too.

"The average player's ego tells him he must be in the starting five to feel important. But my starting five weren't the ones on the court when the game began; they were the ones out there when it mattered most, at the end, when you needed cool heads and steady hands. Most teams start their five best players. I didn't do that."

Instead, he pioneered the "Sixth Man" role with Ramsey.

"After five or six minutes everyone starts getting a bit weary. That's when substitutions begin. So while the opposition would decrease its efficiency by bringing in a lesser talent, we would increase ours by bringing in a Ramsey who'd either maintain the tempo or turn it up a notch." Stats were not mentioned in Auerbach's world, save for one.

"The only stat that counts is winning. I told every one of my guys their salaries depended on what I could see with my own eyes and on what they contributed to the success of the Celtics. That's why I never wanted owners controlling the salaries. Too many guys break their necks at home when they know the owner's watching, then relax when they go on the road. I would remind them that contributions do not mean statistics. No one was ever paid on the basis of points or rebounds, only on what he did to make us a better team. That's all I cared about. We won seven of our championships without having a single Celtic among the league's top 10 scorers. People seem to have this idea that if a man isn't putting points on the board he must be a second-rate member of the cast. That's as ridiculous as saying if you're not shooting, you're not having fun. The fun part of basketball isn't shooting; the fun part is winning."

He was masterful at motivating his troops. "Red was very wise," Satch Sanders said. "He always stressed how strong we were. He never frightened us with reports of how great and strong the other team might be. He believed in a totally positive approach."

Auerbach also understood a good salesman knows when to stop.

CBS "Round Ball" animation figure

It became one of the NBA's first recognized traditions—Red Auerbach lighting up his victory cigar courtside when the Celtics had a victory in hand. The game need not be over. Something in Red's mind said the Celtics were home free . . . and he lit up. Celtics fans—and foes—began looking for the cigar as soon as the Celtics built a healthy lead.

FOLLOWING SPREAD:

Red Auerbach has collected much more than championships during his storied career. His office is a museum of Celtics memorabilia. The collection includes a life-size cutout of Red, a pair of seats from Boston Garden, the 1986 NBA championship trophy, Red's collection of letter openers, assorted photos, proclamations and artists' renderings and, at right, the huge collage of great moments in Celtics history put together by Red's brother, Zang.

The pride and passion for being a Celtic burns brightest in the man whose will and wisdom are forever indelibly linked to the Celtics dynasty. From the day he arrived in 1950 to become coach of a near-bankrupt operation, Arnold "Red" Auerbach devoted himself to the success of the Boston Celtics. He coached nine world championship teams and helped fashion all 16 banners above the parquet floor. On a more personal level, Auerbach was more than willing to argue directly with referees in defense of Celtics virtue.

"The worst thing that can happen to a coach is to fall in love with the sound of his own voice. He becomes successful and now he wants to become an orator, too. So I'd vary the time I spoke, sometimes long, sometimes short, sometimes loud, sometimes soft, and sometimes I wouldn't say much at all. I didn't want to become predictable."

Auerbach was also good at picking his spots. "I never yelled at rookies. And when we lost I rarely said much. I figured they felt bad enough. The worst times I blew my top were when we played lousy and still won. That's when I'd let them have it. Why? Because that would get them ready for the next game."

But before he could get his players ready he first had to get himself ready, which is how his love affair with Chinese food began.

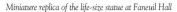

Miniature replica of the life-size statue at Faneuil Hall

"Back in college a professor convinced me the best way to go into an exam was a little bit hungry; that way your mind operates better. Eat a big meal and you feel lethargic, complacent. I never wanted to feel lethargic on the sidelines. I wanted to feel like a tiger—alert, aggressive, maybe even a little bit hostile. So I'd eat lightly early in the afternoon and that would be it until after the game." Chinese restaurants were open late and their steamed fare digested easily, which was why Red incorporated them into his game plan.

The four cornerstones of the Celtics legacy—the spectacular playmaker, the greatest center ever, the architect, and the visionary. As Bob Cousy signs a game ball, Bill Russell, coach Red Auerbach, and founder Walter Brown look on.

He had a reason for everything he did, like grueling training camps that sent the Celtics into their schedule in midseason condition. "Some organizations build teams to make the playoffs," he explained. "We don't think that way. We build teams to win them. So I figured if we opened the schedule in midseason shape we'd steal a lot of games early, then let everyone else try to catch us later."

There was also a reason his Celtics stood during timeouts. "It was a way to psyche the other club. *They* were tired, *they* needed rest, not us. It was like Muhammad Ali standing in his corner between rounds, staring in disgust at an opponent so weak he had to sit on a stool. Do not underestimate the psychological value of that."

Auerbach even discussed referees in his pre-game talks.

"I made it my business to know all I could about every referee, to analyze his personality and anticipate the way he might call a game. So if we had someone like Borgia on the road I'd tell the guys not to challenge him or antagonize him, because I knew he had guts and wouldn't allow the home crowd to intimidate him. It all went into our thinking."

Red Auerbach's success was no accident.

"A lot of coaches, perhaps jealous, felt Red won only because his players were so superior," Jerry West said. "But you can't take outstanding talents, just throw them together and come up with the kind of results Red did. No, he possessed something special. I know for a fact all of his players didn't love him. But they all respected him and that's the word that matters most. Red always had their respect and he always had mine, too."

To Auerbach's way of thinking, there is no higher praise.

"I'd rather hear that than all of the other accolades," he admits.

Red still hears it often, every time the story of the Celtics is told, and well he should because he was exactly what Russell said he was, the best coach in the history of professional sports. ☘

It's not difficult to guess which team won this game. If the cigar isn't a big enough clue, notice the grin on Red Auerbach's face. The occasion is the sixth game of the 1982 Eastern Conference finals in Philadelphia. The Celtics have just defeated the 76ers 88-75 to force a decisive seventh game back in Boston. Auerbach leans against a wall outside the Celtics locker room at the Spectrum, savoring the victory.

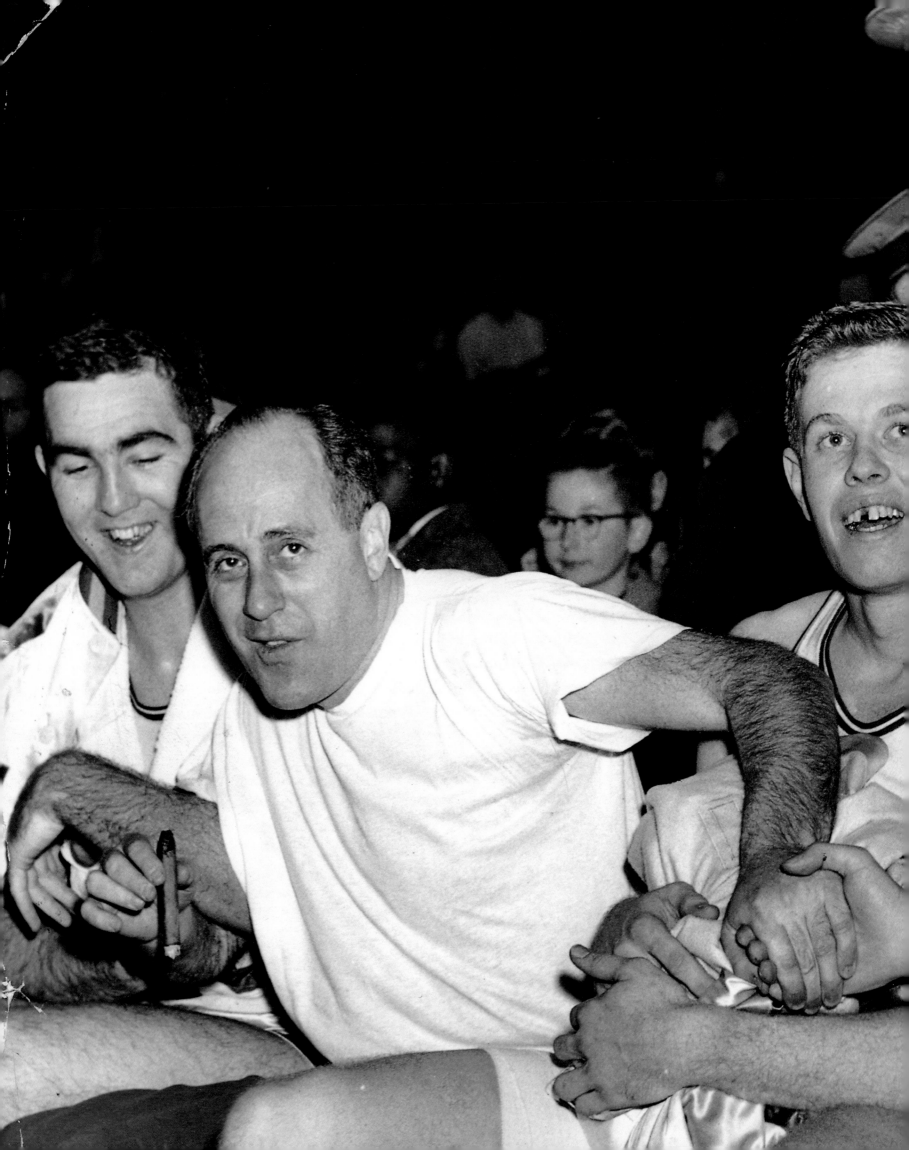

Playing to Glory

"There's no substitution for winning, none. Never forget that."

Red Auerbach

THE
CHAMPIONSHIPS

"Ladies and gentlemen, here come the World Champion Boston Celtics!"

That call, thundering to the rafters where the banners flew, summoned the defending champions of basketball. Onto the parquet they jogged as the organist pumped out "It's a Great Day Tonight for the Irish!"

1956-57

It was the season that launched sports' greatest dynasty, one that would sputter only twice in 13 years. It began with the Celtics acquiring 6-foot-10 William Fenton Russell, who would revolutionize basketball and in 1980 be voted the NBA's greatest player ever, and it concluded with a storybook ending that was one of the great games in basketball history.

"Russ was the guy we desperately needed, our missing link," Red Auerbach says. "And he turned out to be all I expected and more—the greatest of them all, the best basketball player who ever lived." And what Garden fans saw when Russell returned from Melbourne with his Olympic gold medal and played his first NBA game—a 95-93 victory over St. Louis on December 22—was a messiah.

PRECEDING SPREAD:

This is a special moment in Celtics history. Owner Walter Brown, right, player Frank Ramsey, and Red Auerbach, cigar in hand, get ready to celebrate as the Celtics close in on their first division title ever during the first championship season of 1956-57.

Russell used a kangaroo leap and octopus reach to reap a harvest of rebounds and blocked shots to unfurl the fast-break, demoralizing and wearing out opponents while delighting Boston fans. The Celtics were in first place when Russell joined them with a 16-8 record (including a 10-game winning streak). Now, with Russell aboard and Frank Ramsey back from his army hitch, there would be no catching the Celtics. They ran off an eight-victory streak to build their record to 31-14.

Coasting home with a best-in-league 44-28 record for their first division crown by six games over Syracuse, the Celtics continued to roll in the playoffs. Syracuse was wiped out in three straight. Then came St. Louis in the championship series that would be a tense and furious one, a sizzler.

Game 1 in Boston set the tone, an overtime shootout won by the Hawks, 125-123. But the Celtics won Game 2 by 20

1957 Championship ball

points to send the series to St. Louis tied. The teams went on to split the next four games, and the series came down to a seventh-game showdown at the Garden.

It was a classic final game with an unexpected twist for the Celtics. Their proven marksmen, Bill Sharman and Bob Cousy, proved human by going ice cold as rookies Tom Heinsohn (37 points, 23 rebounds) and Bill Russell (19 points, 32 rebounds) saved the day. Russell blocked five shots and dazzled fans during a spectacular and pivotal four-second span midway through the final minute of regulation. Jack Coleman drove for a layup that could have given St. Louis a 3-point lead when Russ swooped in from midcourt and swatted away the ball, then sprinted to the other end and scored a basket giving the Celtics the lead. Bob Pettit sent the game into overtime with two free throws. And a Coleman jumper with nine seconds left in the first overtime spelled double-OT when Sharman's answering shot clanged off the rim. After Heinsohn fouled out, Ramsey's 20-footer gave the Celtics the lead as the clock wound down—slowly, the final 72 seconds taking 10 minutes to complete. And after Jim Loscutoff made a free throw, it was Boston 125, St. Louis 123—with one second left.

Hawks player-coach Alex Hannum inserted himself into the lineup and hurled the ball the length of the floor off the Boston backboard and into the waiting hands of Pettit in the foul lane. The superstar flipped it back up in the same motion but the ball skidded off the rim as the buzzer sounded.

The Celtics finally were world champions, and seeming half of Boston poured onto the parquet and mobbed its heroes. Russell and Loscutoff beat the fans to Red Auerbach, hoisting him to their shoulders before he could light his sweetest victory cigar.

As they celebrated their second title in three seasons, the Celtics couldn't know they had laid the foundation for a dynasty. The 1959 team that triumphed over Minneapolis was the first of eight straight Celtics world champions.

1958-59

There he stood, soaking wet in the Celtics' dressing room at the Minneapolis Armory, trying to draw on a soggy cigar.

"We set a lot of records this season, and some may be broken some day," Red Auerbach hoarsely told the writers, half-shouting to be heard above the celebration after being dunked under a shower. "But one won't be—winning the championship in four straight games.

The 1958–59 Celtics had won their third straight Eastern crown in a runaway. They set a league record for most victories while hammering out a 52-20 record to win the division by a dozen games. Their most-ever 116.4-point average was more than six points a game higher than any other team. The Celtics were a scoring machine that shredded NBA records all season. And none of those peaks was more flabbergasting than a 173-139 victory over the Lakers that would be probed by the league president and still remains one of the highest-scoring games in NBA history.

"It's never been done in basketball before. And it's only what these guys deserve. People have been talking about them being the greatest basketball team of all time. Well, they proved it, didn't they, sweeping through four games? What a bunch!"

They were a bunch who had chafed all season, determined to regain their NBA championship lost in the previous year's finals. Now the crown was theirs again after the stunning 4-0 blitz of the Lakers. The Celtics punctuated the sweep by giddily carrying Auerbach off the court minutes earlier following the clinching 118-113 victory.

Appropriately, Walter Brown was there, making a rare road appearance, and the owner went from Celtic to Celtic shaking hands and thanking his troops. "Sorry you had to play so much," Brown said to Bill Russell, who had ripped down 30 rebounds, including five in the final moments to preserve the victory. "I'm not sorry, I enjoyed it!" Russell replied. "Anytime you're on a great team like this you enjoy staying on the floor."

Russell and the other veterans were saying yes, this title was special, but in a different way from the 1957 championship. That had been a thrill because it was their first; this was a thrill because it was regaining something lost—and doing it in that record four straight.

And across the corridor, in the Laker locker room, numbed coach Johnny Kundla was announcing his resignation—and taking the memory of the powerhouse Celtics with him. "If they stay healthy," he told reporters, "it's going to be a long time before that team gets beaten."

A dynasty was taking root.

1959-60

Media from around the country flocked to the Garden on November 7, 1959, to cover a historic duel, back-dropped against a battle-of-the-undefeated—the Philadelphia Warriors at 5-0, the Celtics at 3-0. Fans jammed the building to overflowing to see the long-awaited confrontation between the Celtic, Bill Russell, who had revolutionized defense in his three pro seasons, and the Warrior, Wilt Chamberlain, the rookie who most predicted would revolutionize offense—and perhaps destroy basketball in the process.

If anyone could stop 7-foot-something Wilt (The Stilt) Chamberlain it would be William Felton Russell, despite spotting him at least four inches.

And when the Warriors came onto the floor for warm-ups, fans ringed the court and *oohed* and *aahed* as Chamberlain stuffed the ball through the basket, seemingly ramming his arms down through the hoop to his elbows. Wilt had popularized the dunk, and, with at least 280 pounds of velocity behind it, it appeared unstoppable. His fallaway jumper from 10–15 feet seemed only slightly less lethal.

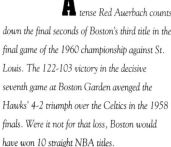

Tom Heinsohn's jersey

The Celtics survived Chamberlain this night, jumping to a 22-7 lead and easing to a 115-105 victory. Chamberlain outscored Russell, 30-22, but Russell had more rebounds, 35-28. And the crowd was ecstatic when Russell climbed an invisible stepladder to block one of his taller foe's shots.

It was the beginning of a classic rivalry that would continue through the sixties. (And at decade's end, Russell would bury Chamberlain by a 3-1 landslide in a vote for NBA Player of the Sixties.)

While that first Russell-Chamberlain duel was spectacular enough, *Sports Illustrated* reported that the show had been stolen by Bob Cousy, who had "displayed a dozen sleight of hand tricks with the basketball that no one had ever seen before. He set up his teammates for scores all night and made 24 points."

Cousy would average a career-high 9.5 assists that season, leading the league for the eighth straight time, and became the first NBA player to chalk up more than 5,000 career assists. And Russell snared an NBA record 51 rebounds while scoring 23 points during a February game against Syracuse at Boston.

A tense Red Auerbach counts down the final seconds of Boston's third title in the final game of the 1960 championship against St. Louis. The 122-103 victory in the decisive seventh game at Boston Garden avenged the Hawks' 4-2 triumph over the Celtics in the 1958 finals. Were it not for that loss, Boston would have won 10 straight NBA titles.

The Bill Russell-Wilt Chamberlain duels that are remembered as the classic battle-of-the-giants matchups of the '60s began with the 1959-60 season, climaxing in the Eastern Conference finals. Russell's Celtics would eliminate Wilt's Warriors 4-2. Chamberlain got his points, but Russell won the war with defense.

Meanwhile, the Celtics were ruling the victory column, winning 11 of their first 12 games before running off a record-equaling 17-victory streak that left them 30-4 by New Year's—rolling on to an NBA record 59-16 finish, 10 games ahead of runner-up Philadelphia. The Celtics' 124.5-point scoring average that season still ranks as their all-time best.

After more Chamberlain-vs.-Russell drama in the hectic Eastern Finals as the Celtics eliminated Philly in six games, the championship series seemed almost anticlimactic, although it seesawed the full seven-game distance. For their third NBA title in four years, the Celts faced the St. Louis Hawks now coached by old friend Easy Ed Macauley. After the series went 1-1, 2-2, and 3-3, the Celtics broke open the finale with a 41-23 second period for a 70-53 halftime lead, and it was all over as Russell triggered one fastbreak after another in the 122-103 victory.

Frank Ramsey had contributed a game-high 24 points and 13 rebounds, Heinsohn scored 22 points and Cousy 19 points and 14 assists. But Russell had been devastating with 35 rebounds and 22 points in a performance opposing superstar Bob Pettit described afterward as "one of the truly great games of all time."

1960-61

"This is the greatest team ever assembled," Red Auerbach said after the Celtics had won their third consecutive championship by again eliminating the St. Louis Hawks at the Garden.

The Celtics had won their division by 11 games with a best-in-the league 57-22 record to annex a fifth straight Eastern title. Then they had thumped Syracuse and St. Louis, each with 4-1 dispatch, to hoist their fourth NBA flag in five years.

In what would be his Celtics farewell, 35-year-old Bill Sharman went out in style in the playoffs—including scoring 30 and 27 points against Syracuse while hounding Hal Greer and Dick Barnett through that series.

And another Bill named Russell scored 25 points, swept 33 rebounds and blocked six shots as the Celts eliminated the Nats. "I put Bill Russell in another world as a basketball player," Syracuse coach Alex Hannum said afterward. "There's nobody like him. Nobody."

The Hawks proved no more of a test than the Nats despite new coach Paul Seymour having run them all the way to a 51-28 record, St. Louis' most wins ever, and then to a 4-3 victory over the Lakers in the Western Finals.

Boston and St. Louis were meeting for the title for the fifth time in six years, but this one was no contest. The Celtics destroyed the Hawks by 34 points in the opener, 129-95, with seven Celtics scoring in double figures, and the series was essentially over.

The Celtics rang up another world championship with a 121-112 victory over the befuddled Hawks as Russell collected 38 rebounds and 30 points. "Russell never stopped," Seymour said afterward. "Every time I looked, he was dunking shots, blocking shots, playing every guy on the floor at one time or another, just to let them know who he was. It's the same old story: he's a big man in a big game."

1961-62

It all came down to five-eighths of an inch, the width of a basketball rim.

The score is tied at 100, and five seconds remain on the Garden clock in the seventh game of the NBA's first coast-to-coast championship series: the Celtics versus the now *Los Angeles* Lakers. It is a fork in the road of Celtics history. It's the Lakers' ball, and if they score the dynasty will end at three.

"It was a madhouse in the huddle," Laker Hot Rod Hundley would recall. "Then the buzzer blew and that great crowd was hushed. Oh, my God, here we go. We had it in our hands. One basket and we're the champs. Five seconds—a lifetime."

The shot figures to be taken by Jerry West or Elgin Baylor. Instead Hundley spots Frank Selvy open to the left of the Celtics basket. With two ticks left on the clock, Selvy hurries a jumper. The ball hits the front rim, skips across the open hole, strikes the back rim—and *falls off*.

Bill Russell is mobbed on the floor of Boston Garden after the Celtics defeated the Los Angeles Lakers 110-107 in overtime of the seventh and deciding game to win a fourth straight championship in 1962. Russell had just completed one of the greatest performances in NBA history, scoring 30 points and pulling down 40 rebounds while playing the entire 53 minutes. His rebound of a miss by Laker Frank Selvy with two seconds to go sent the game into overtime. Russell then scored four of the Celtics' 10 points in the extra session.

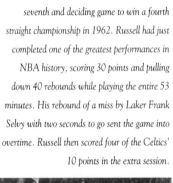

There were certainly bigger, taller and stronger centers in the NBA than Bill Russell. But no one could match the Celtic legend's unique combination of athleticism, timing, and grace under fire.

FOLLOWING SPREAD:

To win their fifth Championship, the Celtics had to go to overtime of the seventh and decisive game before defeating the Los Angeles Lakers 110-107 on April 18, 1962 in Boston Garden. Celebrating the victory are, back row from left, Carl Braun, Bob Cousy, Satch Sanders, Red Auerbach, Frank Ramsey, Tom Heinsohn, Sam Jones and Jim Loscutoff. In the foreground, from left, are Bill Russell, K.C. Jones and a waving Gene Guarilia.

Bill Russell was in orbit, pouncing on the rebound, wrapping both arms around the ball and hugging it as the buzzer sounded. "I nearly had a heart attack watching Selvy's shot," Russell recalls. "Everything was riding on it. When it bounced off the rim I just grabbed it and hung on for dear life." The dynasty was still alive—at least for a five-minute overtime.

This was the Celtics' second consecutive playoff series to come down to the final second of the seventh game at Boston. So had the Eastern Finale against the Philadelphia Warriors two weeks earlier, when Sam Jones' 18-footer with two seconds left gave the Celtics a 109–107 lead that Russell preserved by batting away a long inbounds pass to Wilt Chamerlain camped under the Boston basket.

The Celtics had won 60 games while running away with the division title again—by 11 games over runner-up Philadelphia for the second year in a row.

While the Celtics had stormed to a record victory total during the regular season, the playoffs would prove the toughest of any they had ever won—14 memorable games including the two series-deciders that remain classics in Celtics history.

Bob Cousy's warm-up jacket

Now it's Game 7 overtime against the Lakers and Russell is everywhere, continuing the exhaustless perpetual motion that is making him the Celtics' playoff leader in scoring (22.4 average) as well as rebounds (26.4). In the opening minute, Frank Ramsey becomes the fourth Celtic to foul out trying to cover Elgin Baylor—joining Tom Heinsohn, Tom Sanders, and Jim Loscutoff on the sidelines. Gene Guarilia, a little-used forward, is sent into the game by Red Auerbach.

Guarilia does the job. He feeds Russell for a resounding stuff, collects a rebound and, with two minutes remaining, harasses Baylor into a dis-qualifying sixth foul. Baylor receives a thundering ovation usually reserved for Celtics heroes as he walks back to the Laker bench, his season ended with a 41-point, 22-rebound performance.

With Baylor goes Los Angeles' last hope. The Celtics have a five-point advantage—the lead having changed hands for the 13th and final time—and hold off the Lakers. Cousy dribbles out the last 20 seconds and it's all over: *Boston 110, Los Angeles 107*. After two seventh-game scares, the Celtics are still champions—for a record fourth straight time.

The Garden erupts in its annual spring ritual. Russell is mobbed after playing every second of the game's 53 minutes while totaling 40 rebounds (25 in one half) and 30 points (4 in overtime and, overall, 14 of 17 free throws) to set or tie a variety of NBA and club records. Tears are rolling down Russell's cheeks. And in the locker room, he sits in a corner, the tears still coming. "Well," he says finally, "I'm glad *that's* over."

1962-63

It was the Year of The Cooz—Bob Cousy's last hurrah. At age 34, the hypnotic dribbler, dazzling pass-er, inventive playmaker, and deadly sharpshooter was retiring from the Celtics after 13 seasons.

Around the league, fans poured into arenas for one final look at the 6-foot-1 David who had become a legend in a sport of Goliaths. And through it all, the Celtics captain had one final goal: to go out a winner.

The Celtics breezed to a seventh straight division pennant, 10 games ahead of Syracuse with a best-in-NBA record of 58-22. And that regu-lar season was capped on the final day—St. Patrick's Day—by Bob Cousy Day at Boston Garden. It was a tearful farewell later labeled the Boston Tear Party. That's when, as Cousy tried to compose himself during the emotional halftime ceremonies, the upper balcony-fan bellowed the instantly classic "We love ya, Cooz!"

Like other Celtic greats, Tom Heinsohn had that rare ability to perform at an even higher level during the playoffs. In nine seasons with the Celtics, Heinsohn averaged 18.6 points and 8.8 rebounds per game. In nine years of post season play, Heinsohn averaged 19.8 points and 9.2 rebounds a game. Eight of Boston's world championships came with Heinsohn, shown driving against St. Louis, at forward. He added two more world titles as coach.

The Cincinnati Royals pushed the Celtics to the seven-game limit in the Eastern Finals before Cousy helped fire the Celtics to a back-to-the-wall victory in the clincher with 21-point, 11-assist brilliance. Cousy's determination to win again pushed the Celtics to glory in the last game of the NBA finals against the Lakers. Ahead 3-2 in the series, the Celts were leading by nine points with 10:57 remaining when Cousy, who had scored

Sam Jones was one of the most graceful players of his era. He was quick enough to cut through defenses on the drive, then pull up and make jumpers with uncanny accuracy. His trademark became shots from the side that kissed lightly off the backboard. He played on 10 Celtics world championship teams, including eight in a row.

18 points, went down near midcourt with torn foot ligaments. In obvious pain, Cooz was assisted off the floor—his arms draped around the shoulders of Jim Loscutoff and trainer Buddy LeRoux—as the Los Angeles Sports Arena thundered with what figured to be his farewell.

To the crowd's amazement, Cousy returned with 4:43 left and rallied the fading Celtics to a 112-109 victory. Fittingly, the captain dribbled out the final seconds before heaving the basketball to the rafters as the buzzer signaled the Celtics' fifth straight NBA championship—and Cooz's last, the end of an era.

1963-64

"I think we'd won in 1963 because it was Cooz's last season, and I think we won in 1964 because we were playing *without* Bob," Red Auerbach recalls. "We had something to prove."

The Celtics made their point—emphatically. Moving into the lineup in place of Cousy, K. C. Jones contributed a stout defense and dealt the third-most assists in the league while quarterbacking the world's most famous fastbreak. And although John Havlicek never started a game, the perpetual-motion sophomore led the team in scoring with a 19.9-point average while taking over the retiring Frank Ramsey's role as basketball's best sixth man.

But it was a new pressing defense—made relentless by Bill Russell, Tom Sanders, K. C. Jones, and Havlicek—that made the Celtics devastating. "That was easily the best defensive team we ever had—and maybe the best of all time," Russell says. "Maybe that's why it rates as my favorite team."

"We changed our game and concentrated more on defense," Auerbach explains, "figuring we'd have enough offense if we pitched in and helped Russell shut off the opposition. And it worked, the pressing defense setting up offensive opportunities. We won 59 games (four more than Cincinnati in NBA East), one short of our league record. Then in the playoffs we rolled by two pretty darn good teams—Cincinnati and San Francisco. It was Ramsey's and Loscutoff's turn to go out winners."

The NBA title was the Celtics' sixth in a row as they became the first pro team in any sport to win six successive world championships.

Future Georgetown coach John Thompson played on the Celtics' championship teams of 1965 and '66. Here he is on the floor with Mel Counts (11), Ron Bonham (21) and John Havlicek (17).

The Celtics had made their point—and none more so than Russell, who considers that season his best even though it was the only one in a five-year stretch that he wasn't selected MVP. Among other achievements, he averaged nearly 25 rebounds (and 15 points) a game—1,930 rebounds in all, the most of his career, while escaping Cooz's shadow.

1964-65

It would be known forever after as "The Year Havlicek Stole the Ball." It was the season that the Celtics' dynasty was nearly ended, incredibly, by a guy wire that supported a backboard at the Garden. But the reign was preserved by the most famous play in Celtics history, immortalized by Johnny Most's rasping rhetoric, *"Johnny Havlicek stole the ball!"*

HAVLICEK STEALS THE BALL

APRIL 15, 1965

I couldn't believe it when Havlicek broke up that pass-in. I lost my voice. I couldn't open my mouth."

RED AUERBACH

"All hell broke loose at the Garden," John Havlicek recalls. "The fans swarmed onto the court and began clawing away at me. They started tearing at my jersey and ended up ripping the stirrups off my shoulders. I actually got a rope burn from each one and was bleeding from the collarbone. They got the jersey off by the time I'd reached the exit sign, and by the time I got to the corridor they'd pulled my pants down around my knees. That's how wild it got. And four years later, at Sam Jones' retirement party, a woman came up to me. She was wearing something that looked like a broach attached to her dress."

"'Do you know what this is?' she asked. 'Looks like a piece of rag,' I told her."

"And she said, 'That's part of your jersey from the night you stole the ball.'"

The season was prefaced by the death of Walter Brown. Number 1 was retired for the Celtics founder, raised to the Garden rafters on open-ing night, and the team dedicated the season to him. Wearing black mourning patches sewn on their left shoulder straps, the Celtics roared to their ninth straight NBA East pennant, eclipsing their own league record for most victories—winning 62 against only 18 losses. Runner-up Cincinnati trailed by *14* games.

Acquired at midseason, Wilt Chamberlain rallied the 76ers to a 40-40 finish, making them a playoff threat that quickly eliminated Cincinnati, 3-1. Philadelphia and Boston had split 10 regular-season games, and the seesaw pattern continued in the Eastern Finals. It was a sizzling series tied at 1-1, 2-2, and 3-3 as it alternated between the two cities—each team winning before its rabid home fans.

The series came down to a seventh-game showdown at Boston. The game would decide the Eastern representative to the NBA finals.

The Celtics came out charging and took an 18-point lead after just eight minutes. But the Sixers rallied to take a 62-61 lead. Boston regained the lead, 90-82, going into the fourth period. And the Celts still led by seven points, 110-103, with about a minute left when Auerbach lit his victory cigar. "We had the game locked up," he would say later. "No way we were going to lose it."

The Celtics grew cautious and allowed Chamberlain six straight points to bring the Sixers within one with five seconds remaining. Russell took the ball out of bounds under Boston's basket. Harassed, the 6-foot-10 veteran backed up a half step and jumped as he tried to inbound the ball with both arms upstretched over his head. The ball traveled only inches before striking the overhead guy wire that supported the basket, caroming out of bounds. "Russell lost the ball off the sup-port!" Most screamed into his microphone. Stunned, Russell was still beneath the guy wire but now was kneeling on one knee, pounding the floor with his fist and repeating, "Oh, my God . . . oh, my God . . ." He looked at his teammates and implored, "Somebody bail me out. I blew it."

If the Boston bench was in shock, the Philadelphia bench was in chaos as every Sixer seemed to be making a play for a game-winning bas-ket that would finally dethrone the Celtics.

Coach Dolph Schayes decided to have Hal Greer inbound the ball deep to Chet Walker outside, then take a return pass and put up a quick one-hander from the corner. Harassed, Greer hesitated before finally lobbing the ball toward Walker about 25 feet away near the top of the key. That's when Johnny Havlicek turned his head in time to see the ball arching toward Walker, Hondo uncoiled, leaped into the air and slapped the ball away. And from high above courtside Johnny Most erupted: ". . . *and Havlicek steals it! Over to Sam Jones. Havlicek stole the ball! It's all over! It's alllll over! Johnny Havlicek is being mobbed by the fans! It's alllll over! Johnny Havlicek stole the ball!*"

Russell rushed to Havlicek, hugged him, and pinned a hurried kiss on his forehead before the surging crowd swept its hero away.

1965–66

It was marked a special season from the start, and lived up to expectations.

Arnold Auerbach was coaching one final year before retiring from the bench at age 48 to concentrate on general managing. The Celtics had won "one for Cousy" and for other retiring Celts while collecting past championships; now it was time to win "one for Red."

Auerbach had announced his plans before the season so old rivals could take one last shot at dethroning him and his champions. And in one town after another, opponents and fans around the NBA made final salutes to Red—often breaking out cigars as a good-natured needle for the man they loved to hate during his 20 NBA seasons.

FOLLOWING SPREAD:

Larry Siegfried could slice to the basket, but is even better remembered for his tenacious, aggressive defense and an all-out style that had him diving recklessly for loose basketballs. "I was a tough man to beat in the trenches," said the veteran of five Celtics world championships.

"A loose ball was my ball."

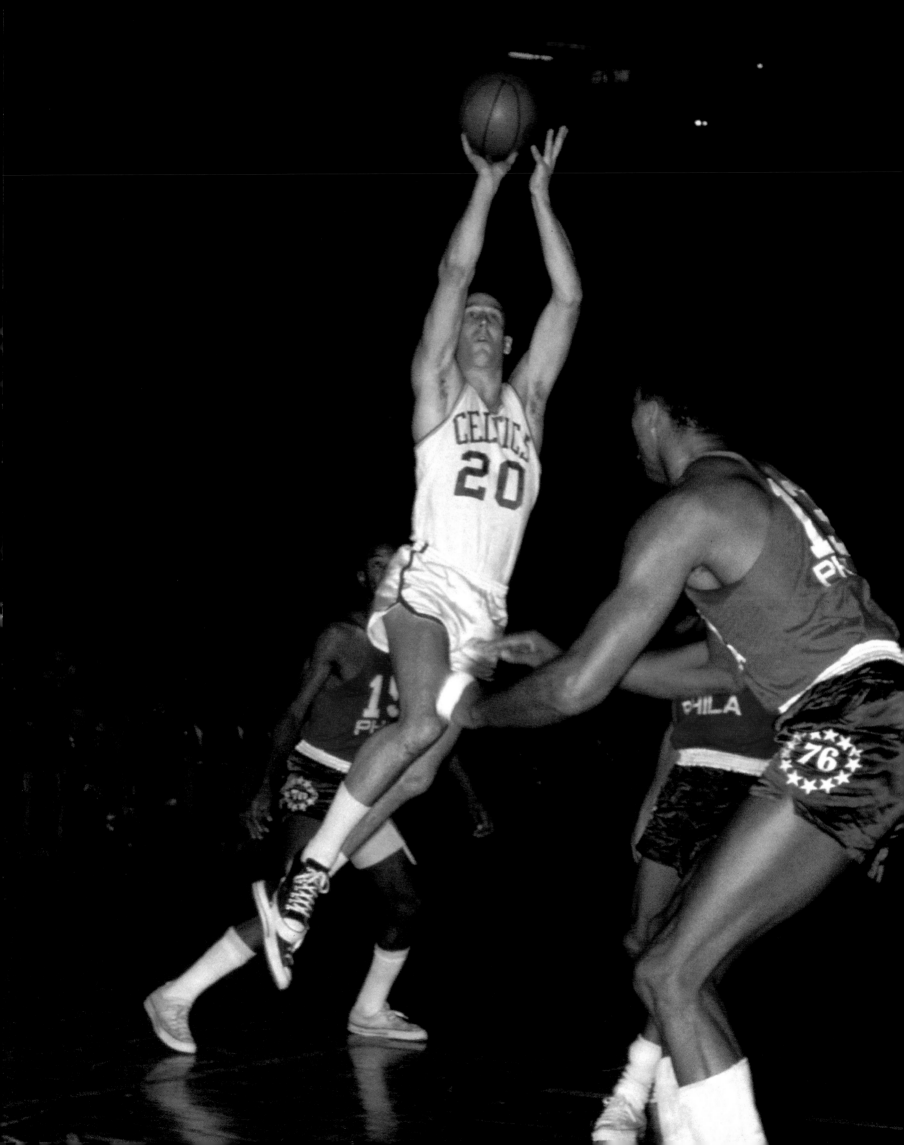

      In his final two seasons with the Celtics, Bill Russell led Boston to NBA championships in 1967–68 and 1968–69 in the grueling dual capacity as player-coach. Russell succeeded Red Auerbach as coach starting with the 1966–67 campaign. Despite inheriting an aging team, Russell's three-season coaching record of 162-83 (.661) ranks him fourth among Celtics coaches in winning percentage behind K. C. Jones, Bill Fitch, and Auerbach, Here Russell discusses strategy with Tom Sanders (16), Sam Jones (24), and John Havlicek (17) during a postseason timeout. Russell retired as a coach when he retired as a player.

Cincinnati's Royals nearly slipped Auerbach a loaded stogie in the playoffs after Boston had finished second in the East, one game behind the 55-25 Philadelphia 76ers, the first time in 10 years the Celtics didn't win the division. Boston was on the verge of elimination from the playoffs as the Royals won two of the first three games in the best-of-five series. But the Celts survived the scare by winning the next two, including the 112-103 finale as Sam Jones scored a clutch 34 points.

Between them, Bill Russell and Tom "Satch" Sanders averaged under 25 points a game during their NBA careers. But they proved there is far more to basketball than scoring. And their contributions went far beyond the obvious defense and rebounding. Russell and Sanders played the game with a savvy "feel."

The Celtics gained revenge for Philadelphia having taken their division championship during the regular season by rolling over the 76ers, 4-1, in the Eastern Finals. And, for the fourth time in five years, the NBA title series pitted Boston vs. Los Angeles, and the championship came down to a seventh-game showdown. Again.

With the Garden crowd roaring approval in crescendo, the Celtics jumped to a 10-0 start, held a 53-38 advantage at halftime, led by 19 early in the second half, and were coasting at 76-60 entering the fourth quarter. Only one drama remained—the moment Auerbach would light his final coaching cigar, his trademarked victory signal that delighted friend and infuriated foe.

With four minutes remaining, the Celtics led by 13 amid rising hysteria as the turnaway crowd of 13,909 anticipated Auerbach soon unwrapping his cigar. Within 30 seconds remaining, Bill Russell's spectacular stuff gave Boston a 10-point cushion—the final installment of a 25-point/32-rebound/48-minute going-away present to Auerbach from his successor. Eleven days earlier, Auerbach had picked Russell as his replacement, as a player-coach, so the Celtics could put speculation behind them and get on with the business of winning another championship.

The countdown continued as Massachusetts Governor John Volpe waited by the Celtics bench, armed with a lighter and eager to fire up the Last Cigar.

"Thirty seconds left, and the Celtics are on the verge of their ninth championship," Johnny Most told his radio audience from high above courtside. "The crowd is going berserk!"

Jerry West scored two quick baskets, but Boston still led by six with 16 seconds left, and that was safe enough for Auerbach. He turned toward Volpe and allowed the future US Secretary of Transportation to light him up.

"I never came closer to disaster," Auerbach would later shudder.

The sight of Auerbach lighting up ignited the crowd, and it went wild now, swarming onto the court.

"Havlicek has called time out because he can't get the ball in play. The crowd has surged down the end line," Most shouted hoarsely into his microphone. "They can't finish the ballgame. They can't get the ball in play. The crowd in its delirium and joy has thrown things onto the floor . . . Red Auerbach is being mobbed by fans, players . . . Officials are asking the crowd to *please* pull back. The crowd wants to get at these guys and hug'em. Auerbach has implored the crowd to step back and let them get the ball in play . . . I have never seen anything like this . . . the fans are on the supports of the baskets."

Shooed back by John Havlicek and other Celtics players, spectators still crowded around the Celtics bench, and at times Auerbach had to jump up to see over their heads. And what he saw, unbelievably, was Celtics turnovers—*four* of them as Boston's lead dwindled to 95-91 with six seconds to go as Laker Leroy Ellis took a jump shot.

"It's *good!*" Most screamed. "Four seconds left, and the lead is down to two points!"

John Havlicek's warm-up jacket

For 10 seasons, one was the coach and the other was the player. But the relationship between Red Auerbach and Bill Russell went far beyond player-coach. Theirs was a deeper bond of mutual respect . . . that seemed to grow stronger even in times of disagreement. Russell's skill helped make Auerbach a great coach. And Auerbach designed a system that made the most of Russell's unique talents. Neither underestimated the importance of the other. Here player seeks out coach—and the coach the player—in a heartfelt embrace to celebrate one of their nine championships together. When Auerbach retired from the sidelines after the 1965-66 season, Russell was his hand-picked successor to serve as player-coach through two more championship seasons.

Ellis' basket pulled the plug on crowd noise, and an eerie hush fell over the Garden. Stunned fans knew the shrewd Auerbach had never lit up prematurely. Could that happen now—in Red's final game and spoil his going-away party? Would basketball's winningest coach end his career with an embarrassing loss? Auerbach watched a few feet away as Sam Jones inbounded the ball to K. C. Jones.

"K. C. with the ball, gets surrounded," Most rasped. "One second. *That's it! It's all over!* Havlicek got the pass and he gets mobbed! *It's alllll over!*"

And in an instant, Auerbach was hoisted onto shoulders amid a sea of bobbing heads and transported to the Celtics locker room for the traditional dunking in the showers.

"I feel drunk," the sopping wet Auerbach yelled after his dunking, still embracing the game ball from his 885th Celtics victory and 1,037th NBA triumph, "and I haven't even had a drink!"

Finally, Auerbach exited the Garden for the last time as coach—clad in an old sweatsuit because his clothing was soaked. One final surprise awaited. When Red reached his automobile, a parking ticket decorated the windshield.

Growling, Red Auerbach headed back to his Hotel Lenox suite, whipped up some french fries and ordered a feast of Chinese food. And, finally alone, he cried.

The six championship series between the Celtics and Lakers in the '60s were matches of great players as well as great teams. Here Boston's Satch Sanders races Los Angeles guard Jerry West for a loose ball. The Celtics won all six championship series—three in the decisive seventh game.

1967-68

Ever since the championship streak had ended the previous spring, the number one question around the NBA was: have the Celtics gotten too old?

Then the Celtics launched the season with six victories in a row and a 25-7 start. But they quickly cooled off, going 29-21 the rest of the way as they faded over the long haul and finished a distant second for the second straight year—and by the same eight-game margin.

Wasn't that the answer to everyone's question?

Still, entering the playoffs, there was optimism among the Celtics that they could regain the championship. In the opening round, they swept the final three games to oust the Pistons. The 76ers also had won their semifinal, setting up a Boston-Philadelphia showdown. It was time for revenge. If the Celtics were to regain their lost crown, they would have to wrench it from the head that wore it.

In Game 1, they upset the Sixers convincingly, 127-118, as John Havlicek continued his acceleration toward superstardom with 35 points while Sam Jones added 28 and Bailey Howell 24. But Philly stormed back to win the next three games. It seemed an impossible task for the old, tired, and bruised Celtics to beat the mighty 76ers three straight, especially with two of those games scheduled for Philadelphia. No NBA team had ever lost a seven-game series at any playoff level after leading 3-1.

Don Nelson feared his playing career was at an end before the Celtics signed him as a free agent five games into the 1965–66 season. He played 11 more seasons in Boston and was part of five championship teams. As a player, Nelson was an all-around solid performer who gave the maximum effort. His tenacity served him well after his playing career ended. He became one of the NBA's most successful head coaches.

"Before the next game," Wayne Embry recalls, "John Havlicek and I walked into the locker room and wrote PRIDE on the blackboard in great big letters." Corny? Perhaps, but as Tom Sanders says, "The things other people laughed at, the Celtics believed in." Whatever the stimulus, the Celtics bounced back to humble the 76ers 122-104, and disappoint the Philadelphians who had packed the Spectrum to witness a Celtics guillotining for the second straight year.

"I don't want this season to end," Havlicek said after contributing 29 points and 10 assists while playing all 48 minutes. "In a game like this, if all your guts fall out you just pick them up, stuff them back, and keep going." And the Celtics kept going, winning the next two games including

John Havlicek could do so many things that his rebounding is often overlooked by historians. The 6-foot-5 Havlicek came down with 8,007 rebounds in his career to rank fifth on the Celtics' all-time list.

the 100-96 finale at Philadelphia—dethroning the Sixers in the same city where the Celts had yielded their throne the previous spring.

Now Los Angeles lay in wait, thirsting for its first NBA title while getting even for some of the past Celtics abuse.

The old rivals split the first four games. The Celts then captured the next two—clinching decisively at the new Forum, 124-109—once again frustrating the Lakers. For the third straight series in these playoffs, the Celtics had clinched in the opponent's backyard to regain the title the hard way.

So, for the 10th time in 12 years, the Celtics again were world champions. Their dynasty wasn't over after all.

1968-69

It all came down to one final game—the seventh game of the NBA finals at Los Angeles.

The Lakers had acquired Wilt Chamberlain to team with Elgin Baylor and Jerry West, and were labeled the "greatest basketball team ever assembled." There were forecasts they would run away from the rest of the league. The Celtics, handicapped by old age and the injuries that go with it, struggled to fourth place, their lowest finish in 20 seasons, nine games behind first-place Baltimore in the East.

Sam Jones, the oldest player in the league at nearly 35, announced he'd retire at season's end. Bill Russell, some suspected, would quit after the playoffs. The average age of Boston's eight regulars was a creaking 31. Was there any doubt the Celtics were over the hill? Besides their fourth-place finish, wasn't the succession of injuries that wracked them all season another symptom of old age?

There was a hidden incentive for one Celtic. "About midway through that season I decided that I was playing my last year," Russell would reveal later. "We were hoping to win a last championship for Sam. Privately, I dedicated myself to leaving just as happy as Sam at season's end."

Whatever the motivation, the Celtics breezed through the first two playoff rounds over teams that had finished ahead of them in the standings—eliminating second-place Philadelphia, 4-1, then third-place New York, 4-2. Now came Los Angeles—again.

Tom Heinsohn brought the same fire that made him a great player to the sidelines as Celtics coach as Bill Russell's successor in 1969. In nine seasons, Heinsohn compiled a 427-263 record as coach while leading Boston to five straight Atlantic Division titles and two more NBA championships—1973–74 and 1975–76. Only Red Auerbach won more games as Celtics coach.

Though the Celtics were defending champions, the Lakers were favored. And again, it came down to that seventh-game showdown after the teams divided the first six games, each winning before home fans. Now, the Lakers had the homecourt advantage and their ownership planned a coronation.

A nation watched on ABC as Boston jumped to leads of 17-9 and 24-12. But L.A. closed to 28-25 at quarter's end. The halftime margin was the same, 59-56 Boston. The Lakers tied the score at 60, then went cold, missing 15 shots and not scoring a point for 5 minutes and 24 seconds. The Celtics took advantage to rebuild their lead to 11, and by the final seconds of the third period Boston was up 17, 91-74.

The Lakers closed to nine with 5:30 left on the clock. That's when Chamberlain limped to the sidelines with a hurting knee and took himself out. Mel Counts, the former Celtic, replaced Wilt and the Lakers rallied to within a point, 103-102, with 3:07 remaining. The Forum was vibrating as the aging Celtics faded. Now 80 seconds remained, and with the 24-second clock expiring John Havlicek set for a quick shot. But the ball was knocked loose and picked up by Don Nelson. The ex-Laker's desperation 15-footer struck the back rim, bounded straight up about three feet, then dramatically dropped straight through the hoop—*swish!*

The basket gave the Celtics a three-point cushion for the final 77 seconds, and they improved it to 108-102 before allowing a couple of free throws and a meaningless basket at the buzzer: 108-106. The Celtics' dynasty wasn't dead yet. And of all the 11 world championships so far, in many ways this was the sweetest—hammered out after the Celts had been written off as has-beens.

1973-74

THE CELTICS ARE BACK, the bumper stickers announced.

Tom Heinsohn had rebuilt the new-era Celts into winners as he blended veterans John Havlicek, Don Nelson, and Paul Silas with young Dave Cowens, Jo Jo White, and Don Chaney.

John Havlicek pours champagne into the NBA championship trophy, named for late Celtics owner Walter Brown, during the 1974 victory celebration. Hondo toasted eight championships during his 16 Celtics seasons. But 1974 was extra special— the year he was named the playoffs' MVP while averaging 27.1 points.

It was an exciting team that had been narrowly denied in the previous spring's playoffs after Havlicek crucially injured a shoulder. Now Hondo was mended and the Celtics seemed poised to overtake the aging New York Knicks in the East and proceed to the championship round that had eluded them a year ago.

The Celts put down a stubborn young Buffalo Braves team, featuring Rookie of the Year Ernie DiGregorio and previous Rookie of the Year Bob McAdoo, in six games, then moved down New York state and unseated the Knicks in five.

What followed was to be the classic matchup between a Celtics team of role players with a fiery, scrambling 6-foot-8 1/2 center versus a Milwaukee team with the league's best record (59-23) and their Big Man, 7-foot-2 Kareem Abdul-Jabbar, an all-purpose scorer, rebounder, shot-blocker, and traffic cop.

From series start, the Celtics tried to choke off the Bucks attack before the ball could get to Abdul-Jabbar, pressing relentlessly fullcourt. Trailing 2-1, Milwaukee decided to relieve the pressure on its back-court by switching 6-foot-7 Mickey Davis to guard and having Oscar Robertson bring up the ball. That strategy brought a 97-89 victory at Boston and tied the series. The Celtics spirited away Game 5, 96-87, at Milwaukee and went back home to wrap it up.

Dave Cowens—6-foot-8 1/2-inches and 230 pounds—was a midget among NBA centers. But Cowens routinely out-played superstars bigger and taller and twice led the Celtics to the NBA title. Cowens was the league's Most Valuable Player during a 1972–73 campaign in which he averaged 20.5 points and 16.2 rebounds a game.

From the beginning in Game 6, the Bucks ran up leads of 27-19 and 47-40. It took a fourth-quarter comeback to force an overtime, each team scoring only four points in what Havlicek would label "the finest five minutes of defensive basketball I've ever seen played by two teams." With 1:46 remaining in the second overtime, Havlicek kept the Celtics alive (he'd score 9 of Boston's 15 overtime points). As the second overtime session drew to a close, Havlicek swished two bullseyes from the corner over a menacing Kareem, including the apparent winner with eight seconds to go—101-100.

Havlicek's heroics had put the Celtics on the threshold of the world championship, and the Garden thundered in anticipation. Yet Abdul-Jabbar, with the clock running out and Milwaukee's last-chance play in shambles, found time and space to bring the Bucks back home with a spectacular skyhook, his hallmark, cleanly through—*swish*—with three seconds remaining. And there it was: Milwaukee 102, Boston 101, with the seventh game scheduled for the Bucks' 10,000-seat cockpit of an arena.

TRIBUTES TO CHAMPIONSHIPS

Charm made for players' wives

1959 NBA World Championship tie tack

From the 1956–57 championship season through the championship of 1967–68, rings were awarded to players participating in their first championship. With the exception of the player's name and the year, the ring design was unchanged for each of these championships. No additional rings were given to players for any subsequent championships until 1968–69. For example, Bill Russell, who played on each of the 11 championship teams from 1956–57 through 1968–69 received only two championship rings. Starting with 1968–69, and for each subsequent championship, each player, coach, trainer, team doctor, and member of upper-level management received a ring. The design of the 1973–74 and 1975–76 rings followed the NBA standard differing from earlier Celtics ring designs. The NBA standard design was issued to all championship teams until 1980-81. In that year, the Celtics modified the NBA standard slightly. Since 1983-84, all NBA championship rings have been individually designed by the winning team.

Plate especially commissioned for the 1964
NBA World Championship

1963 NBA World Championship ring

1976 NBA World Championship ring

NBA BASKETBALL

1964

1963

1957

1962

1959

1964

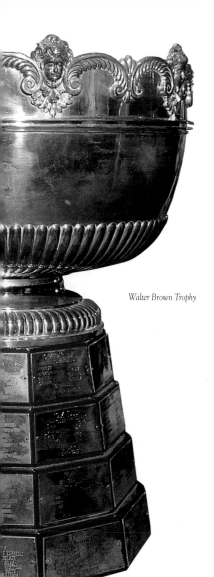

Walter Brown Trophy

1986 NBA World Championship wristwatch celebrating all 16 titles.

1986 NBA World Championship trophy

1957 NBA World Championship ring

1969 NBA World Championship ring

1974 NBA World Championship ring

1984 NBA World Championship ring

1986 NBA World Championship ring

In Game 7, Heinsohn decided to go for broke. The Celtics would sag on Abdul-Jabbar, choking off access to him, and dare the Bucks to shoot from outside. It was a stunning gamble—and it worked perfectly. Sandwiched between Cowens in front and Silas in back, Abdul-Jabbar was held scoreless for nearly 18 minutes through the middle of the game as Boston built a 17-point lead. The Celtics had run away to a 63-46 lead by the time Abdul-Jabbar came up for air in the third quarter. And with 1:34 remaining and the Celts' first NBA championship in five years (and his first as coach) assured, Heinsohn pulled his regulars and Red Auerbach ignited the victory cigar and watched the final touches applied to a sweet 102-87 triumph. Role players and defense, the timeless staples of basketball, had prevailed. And the bumper sticker had been correct.

1975-76

It was the Year of the Triple-Overtime classic, widely considered the greatest NBA game ever played.

The Celtics had cruised through the schedule with the league's second-best record—54-28—and had won the Atlantic Division by eight games over Buffalo despite not having a scorer among the NBA's top 20. Then they had reached the finals with large amounts of guile, tenacity, and rebounding (Dave Cowens and Paul Silas among the league's top four) and a dash of luck.

he Celtics were seeking a shooting guard to replace the retiring Sam Jones when they used their first-round pick in the 1969 draft to select 6-foot-3 Jo Jo White of Kansas. White filled baskets and Celtics expectations. Jo Jo owns the sixth-highest scoring average (18.3) in Celtics history and scored 33 points in a triple-overtime victory over Phoenix in the 1976 finals—leading the Celtics to the championship and earning White the playoff MVP award.

History lay ahead—the three-OT megathriller against Phoenix on a muggy night in June at the Garden. It was decided by the margin of one basket, gave Boston a 3-2 lead in the title series and all but assured the Celtics a 13th—and delightfully unexpected—championship.

"That triple-overtime game was my greatest moment," Jo Jo White said of the 128-126 Picasso to which he contributed 33 points en route to the playoffs' MVP award.

The Celtics had easily won the first two games in Boston, 98-87 and 105-90, but the world turned upside down when they arrived at Phoenix. The Mean 13 (as in 13,000 zealots) at the Coliseum had watched their *"Sunderellas"* defy odds for more than two months, so they were hardly surprised when Phoenix won the next two games, 105-98 and 109-107, and shifted their pressure onto the Celtics' back for Game 5.

There had never been a game like it. From the beginning it belonged to the Celts, who rolled up a 42-40 edge in the second quarter and led, 92-83, with 3:49 to play. Then Paul Westphal, the former Celtic, scored nine of the Suns' next 11 points, including five in a row, to put the game into overtime. And for more than nine minutes—virtually two full five-minute overtimes—the opponents played cautiously, looking for an opening. Then they crammed an evening's worth of dramatics into 19 seconds as Garden fans went on a emotional elevator.

A drive by White gave Boston a 109-106 lead. A jumper by Dick Van Arsdale whittled it to a point. Westphal stole the Celtics' inbounds pass to set up a second-rebound swish by Curtis Perry, and the Suns found themselves ahead. The ball, and final shot, would belong to a familiar hero. John Havlicek's off-balance banker touched off a wild, premature Garden party which quickly turned ugly once the spectators realized that referee Richie Powers, ever in control amid chaos, was insisting the game be played out—and would get slugged for it by a Garden rowdy. Westphal shrewdly drew a calculated technical foul and gave Boston a free throw, giving the Suns the ball at halfcourt instead of at their baseline. With only two seconds left on the clock, that made all the difference.

White's foul shot made it 112-110, but Phoenix forward Gar Heard had time to launch a 22-foot turnaround at the buzzer and it was tied.

Larry Bird skies toward the rim for two points in the 1981 championship series against Houston. The title was the first of three during Bird's run with the Celtics.

The final overtime would be a war of attrition with some unlikely heroes. Jim Ard, replacing fouled-out Cowens, controlled a vital jumpball and later sank the two free throws that equaled the final margin. White added two baskets and Glenn McDonald scored six points after coming in for the disqualified Silas. The Celtics built a 126-120 lead and it was over—both the game and the series. That became official 39 hours later in their 100th game of the season, when they concluded it at Phoenix, the Celtics riding a 17-6 run in the final seven minutes to produce an 87-80 victory and Title No. 13.

"Here we go again," crowed Red Auerbach, his clothes drenched from the shower, smoke billowing from a victory cigar.

1980-81

It was a season replete with Celtic surprises—and revivals.

Dave Cowens stunned the basketball world during the preseason by retiring just before his 32nd birthday. Pete Maravich also suddenly retired, leaving behind a void which underscored lingering questions about the Boston backcourt. It also left Cedric Maxwell, six weeks shy of his 25th birthday, the senior Celtic. Yet the Celtics went on to win the NBA championship.

Vintage Auerbach maneuvering dealt Boston's No. 1 slot in the entire draft to Golden State, which picked up Joe Barry Carroll in return for the Celts picking up fourth-year, 7-foot-1/2 center Robert Parish and 6-foot-10 center-forward Kevin McHale, clearly a master twin stroke in bolstering the frontcourt while not costing a player from the roster. The Red-handed coup took on extraordinary import four months later when Cowens surprisingly quit.

The Celtics' comeback came during the regular season. After falling six games behind division-leading Philadelphia, the Celtics ran off a string of 25 victories in 26 games, culminating in the regular-schedule finale, when the Celtics beat the 76ers, 98-94, at the Garden. The victory gave the Celts a tie for best record in the league at 62-20, the homecourt advantage throughout the playoffs, the Atlantic Division title and a reprieve from facing the 60-22 Milwaukee Bucks in the playoffs.

What was called the advent of the *real* NBA playoffs was destined to take on historic proportions when the Celts and Sixers collided in the Eastern Finals.

Game 1 at Boston saw Philadelphia erase a fourth-quarter Celtics rally. Riding Larry Bird's hot shooting (33 points), the Celts had bounced back from a nine-point deficit with less than three minutes remaining for a 104-103 lead with four seconds to play.

Boston's go-ahead points came on a pair of Bird free throws after a disputed Lionel Hollins foul. Andrew Toney then drove the baseline with two seconds left and was tripped by Maxwell. Toney then coolly sank both free throws for a 105-104 Philly win.

The Celtics had Game 2 won virtually from the opening tapoff. Aware that to lose the first two games of a series at home meant almost certain extinction, Boston used 34 points from Bird—23 in the first half—to fuel the series' only blowout, 118-99.

Cedric Maxwell knew he was hot entering the 1981 Eastern Finals against the Philadelphia 76ers—a series that many NBA fans saw as being for the title. Max was named the playoff MVP for averaging 16.1 points and shooting 58 percent from the floor.

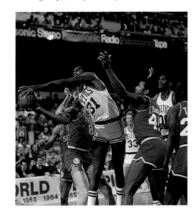

He wasn't the MVP in the 1984 championship, as he had been in 1981, but Cedric Maxwell still played a major role as the Celtics defeated the Lakers 4-3 in the NBA finals. In the locker room before Game 7 at Boston, Max advised teammates, "Hop on my back, boys, and I'll take you on in." In that decisive game, Maxwell delivered, scoring 24 points and adding eight rebounds and eight assists. The first of the Bird-Magic championship series had gone to the Celtics—as had the seven previous Celtics-Lakers title matchups.

The series moved to Philadelphia for Game 3, and the Celtics promptly suffered their 10th straight loss at the Spectrum, 110-100. The Celtics' losing streak in Philadelphia became known as the "Spectrum Jinx" after Game 4 as another late rally by Boston fell short, 107-105, to put the Green in a three-games-to-one hole.

M. L. Carr created havoc on the floor with his aggressive defense. The future Celtics head coach came off the bench to stir the pot for two championship teams, although his greatest efforts as a player probably came in the Eastern Conference finals of 1981.

Striving to be only the fourth team ever to rebound from that deficit in a seven-game NBA series, the Celtics took a giant step in that direction with a finally successful late rally in Game 5 at Boston. But it still came down to the final second. After Julius Erving had fouled in the backcourt, M. L. Carr went to the line with that last tick showing on the clock and sank the first free throw. But he intentionally missed the next two, hoping time consumed by the rebound would end the game.

Darryl Dawkins rebounded the final miss and managed to call time, giving Philadelphia the ball at halfcourt. But Bobby Jones' inbound pass was intercepted by Parish to end it as the ancient Garden echoed in relief.

The prospects for a Philadelphia win seemed likely with the Celtics coming back into the Spectrum pit for Game 6. In the second quarter the 76ers held a 17-point lead, but the Celtics managed to trim it to nine at the half. Then, with 8:10 remaining in the third quarter, the Celtics got their desperately needed spark. Maxwell, called for a loose-ball foul, stumbled out of bounds. On his way back inbounds, a Philadelphia fan taunted Maxwell, and the usually even-tempered Celtic plunged into the stands after his tormentor. The result was an emotional, physical duration as the Celtics and Sixers fought with fierce determination. When Bird dumped in one three-point play, five bodies including his own hit the floor.

With 14 seconds left, the Celtics clinched a trip back to Boston for a seventh game. Rookie Andrew Toney drove on rookie Kevin McHale, who blocked Toney's drive and recovered the ball in midair to seal the Celts' 100-98 win, their first at the Spectrum since January 20, 1979.

The rivals, who both had finished the regular season at 62-20, having split the schedule 3-3 and the playoffs 3-3, would decide the finale by the slimmest of margins. Philadelphia, which had built 11-point leads in the second and third quarters, held an 89-82 edge with 5:23 remaining. With 4:34 left and the Celtics down by six, coach Bill Fitch advised his Boston bench: "We've got them right where we want them." And the Celts did, completing their escape from the brink of defeat with defense, picking off passes, double-teaming the ball, and rotating defenses that held the Sixers basketless the rest of the way.

The game-winner came after Dawkins missed inside. Bird stumbled out with the rebound, streaked down the left side, pulled up 17 feet from the basket, and dropped in a banker with 1:03 on the clock. After the teams exchanged turnovers, Maurice Cheeks was set up with two shots from the free throw line with 29 seconds left. "Don't choke," Carr cautioned, patting Cheeks on the backside. Maurice made only one shot. Boston then ran down the clock until a Carr 22-footer deflected off the rim to Parish—who lost it to Bobby Jones with one second left. With one last chance at redemption, the Sixers had Erving trying to slip open near the basket, but Jones' inbounds pass hit the top of the backboard and the Celtics had their 91-90 victory.

One of the greatest transactions in Celtics history was the acquisition of Dennis Johnson after the 1982–83 season.

"Dennis made everyone on the team more effective—including the coach," says K. C. Jones, who coached the Celtics during Johnson's first five seasons. "He was like having another coach on the floor."

"I know what it takes to win in this league," DJ would say—and proved it game after game. With him at the controls, the Celtics won over 75 percent of their games during his first five seasons: a heady 308-102. And that record would grow to 402-172 before Johnson bowed out two years later.

He had arrived with one diamond ring from Seattle's 1979 championship and added two more in 1984 and 1986 with the Celtics. Shortly after his retirement as a player, Johnson joined the team's scouting and coaching staffs.

The Celtics were back in the NBA finals—this time against the Houston Rockets, a 40-42 team Boston had beaten 13 straight times.

The scene was ripe for a letdown, and that flatness showed in Game 1 at Boston as the Celtics squeezed out a 98-95 victory on superior rebounding. In Game 2, Moses Malone gathered 31 points and 15 rebounds to snap the Celtics' curse over Houston, 92-90. Game 3 was all Boston, 94-71. Houston bounced back in Game 4, 91-86, to even matters at 2-2. The series returned to Boston for Game 5 with Cedric Maxwell, who would be the finals' MVP, leading the way with 28 points and 15 rebounds as the Celts ran away, 109-80.

Back at the Summit for Game 6, the Celtics' 14th championship seemed iced with a 17-point lead early in the fourth quarter. But the Rockets staged one final surge, pulling within three with 2:05 to play. Then Bird (27 points) took over, dumping in a baseline fade, a 20-footer and a three-pointer to put the Celtics up by six, 95-89, en route to their 102-91 coronation.

Robert Parish's jersey

The newest generation in a bloodline of champions had won it. And a new Celtics championship era had dawned.

1983-84

It was like old times. Some of the fans were new, but the rivalry was old. For the first time since 1969, the Celtics were paired again with the Lakers in the NBA finals.

It would feature a dream rivalry within the rivalry—Bird vs. Magic—but first there was the matter of the Knicks and the Bucks.

During the regular season, the Celtics posted a best-in-the-NBA 62-20 record. But they were only 3-3 against 47-35 New York. And they were 3-3 against the Knicks going into the decisive game of the conference semifinals.

The Celtics, the Lakers, the parquet of the Boston Garden. Basketball didn't get any better than this in the '80s. The rivals met three times for the NBA championship. The Celtics prevailed 4-3 in 1984—their eighth straight championship series triumph over the Lakers.

Enter Larry Bird. In the seventh game at Boston, he scored a career playoff high of 39 points while collecting 12 rebounds and distributing 10 assists as the Celtics eliminated the New Yorkers, 121-104.

"Bird's performance was beyond description," Knicks coach Hubie Brown told the media. "I hope nobody underestimates what he did. His game was tough to chart because most of it was from downtown. From the perimeter, he was fantastic."

Next in the Eastern Finals were the Milwaukee Bucks, who had swept the Celtics rudely aside in a four-game sweep in the 1983 division semifinals.

Now it was payback time. This time, it was the Celtics who dominated—winning the first three, dropping one in Milwaukee, then closing out the Bucks at the Garden, 115-108.

The preliminaries over, it was time for the first Celtics-Lakers championship series in 15 years. The rivals had collided for the title seven times and the Lakers had never prevailed. But these were the Lakers of Magic Johnson and Kareem Abdul-Jabbar, Pat Riley's showtime band. The Lakers were nearly as dominant in the West as the Celtics were in the East.

It was a dream-championship matchup pitting basketball's two premier franchises—and featuring the game's two premier players: Bird and Johnson.

"We're not going to get into a personal duel," Johnson insisted. "But everyone knows what I think about Bird. He's the smartest player in the league. That's where he excels . . . combining talent and intelligence."

Clearly, the Lakers were excited. "This is something special," said Riley. "There's great history here. Why not get nostalgic? The ghosts of (Jerry) West and (Bill) Russell and that classic 1969 series lingers in this one."

Gerald Henderson was a pivotal player during the '84 finals vs. Los Angeles. Inserted into the lineup because his speed gave the Boston defense an added dimension, the cry "Henderson steals the ball" was heard down the stretch as the Celtics rallied from a six-point deficit with less than two minutes to go to win the critical fifth game while facing elimination.

It is unlikely the Celtics—or any NBA team—will ever see another combination along the front line like Robert Parish, Kevin McHale, and Larry Bird. They arrived in Boston within the span of a year—and remained through the 1980s and for the Celtics' 14th, 15th, and 16th world championships. Bird arrived first, as the sixth player selected in the 1979 college draft. A year later the Celtics negotiated a trade with the Warriors. In exchange for Boston's top spot in the 1980 draft, the Celtics would get fourth-year center Parish and the Warriors' No. 3 spot in the draft (and selected McHale). Bird (21,791 points) is the Celtics' second all-time leading scorer to John Havlicek. Parish (18,245) is No. 3 on the list, and McHale (17,335) No. 4. Parish (11,051) is second to Bill Russell among the Celtics' all-time rebounders. Bird (8,974) is No. 4, and McHale (7,122) is No. 6.

The Lakers' game was running. The Celtics figured to be bigger and stronger. The edge went to Boston on home-court advantage—which it lost immediately. With Jabbar scoring 32 points and Johnson getting 10 assists, the Lakers stunned the Celtics 115-109 in the opener at Boston despite Bird's 24 points and 14 assists.

Then the Celtics came dangerously close to going down 2-0 at home before a pair of subs came to the rescue. With 13 seconds left in regulation, Gerald Henderson electrified the Garden as he stole a pass and scored to tie the game and force overtime, before Scott Wedman's corner jumper with 14 seconds to play in OT spelled a series-evening 124-121 victory.

Disaster awaited in Los Angeles, where the Celtics were buried 137-104. It was Boston's worst defeat ever in a championship series as Magic set a postseason record with 21 assists.

But the Celts bounced back in Game 4—possibly the most important game in the series—scoring a 129-125 victory as Dennis Johnson collected 22 points and 14 rebounds and hit a series of clutch baskets down the stretch. The win evened the series at 2-2 and returned the homecourt advantage to the Celtics as the teams returned to Boston.

This time the Celtics didn't give up the advantage. Inside the steamy Garden, Boston prevailed 121-103 as Bird hit 15 of his 20 shots from the floor, finishing with 34 points and 17 rebounds.

Back at the Forum, the Lakers rallied from 11 points down to a 119-108 victory that sent the deadlocked series back to Boston for the finale won by the Celtics, 111-102. Championship banner number 15 was headed for the rafters—where it belonged, according to Cedric Maxwell.

"We have a heart as big as this room," the forward told reporters after leading the winners with 24 points, eight rebounds and eight assists. "We are the greatest team in the world right now."

And the battle between Bird and Magic? All Larry. He led all scorers (27.4 points per game) and rebounders (14.0) to be a unanimous selection as series MVP.

1985-86

The Los Angeles Lakers finally had their NBA championship at Boston's expense in 1985—the Lakers triumphing in six games behind Magic. So entering the 1985-86 season, Celtics players and fans were looking toward a rubber match between Johnson's Lakers and Bird's Celtics. It didn't happen.

Boston kept its side of the bargain. The Celtics had a league-best 67-15 during the regular season, an NBA-record 40-1 at home. The Celts then breezed into the NBA Finals with a 11-1 record in the Eastern playoffs after eliminating Michael Jordan and the Chicago Bulls (3-0), Atlanta Hawks (4-1), and Milwaukee Bucks (4-0). But the Lakers didn't reach the dance—routed 4-1 in the Western Finals by the Houston Rockets and their "twin towers," 7-foot Akeem Olajuwon and 7-4 Ralph Sampson.

The Celtics had their own twin towers in 7-foot-1/2-inch Robert Parish and

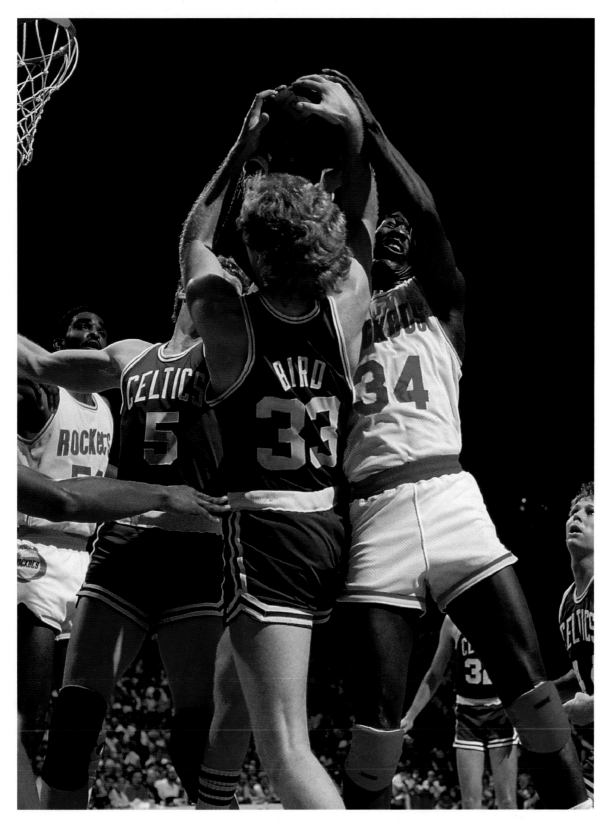

The 1985–86 Celtics, which routed Houston 4-2 in the finals, might be the best Celtics team ever assembled. The starting five featured guards Dennis Johnson and Danny Ainge backed by Kevin McHale, Larry Bird, and Robert Parish, pictured far left. Bird was named MVP of both the regular season and the playoffs. Bill Walton was honored as the league's best sixth man. McHale and Johnson were named to the all-defensive team.

Houston had the tandem of 7-foot Akeem Olajuwon, left, and 7-foot-4 Ralph Sampson, following page. The Celtics countered the Twin Towers with their hard-working frontline.

Boston's upfront quartet averaged 70.5 points, 31.7 rebounds, and 5.7 blocks a game to the Twin Towers' totals of 39.5 points, 21.3 rebounds, and 4.0 blocks a game. "The Celtics always had a fresh body on us," said Sampson. "It took a toll . . . they wore us down."

6-foot-10 Kevin McHale . . . *plus* 6-foot-11 newcomer Bill Walton, healthy for one last run at glory. And the Celtics also had two things the Rockets didn't—Bird and the Garden.

It wasn't a classic finals. But it was physical. That tone was set in the opener won by the Celtics, 112-100. Sampson and Olajuwon both got in foul trouble, although the latter contributed 33 points and 12 rebounds. Sampson drew

the series' first blood with an elbow that swelled Dennis Johnson's eye nearly shut, but DJ still managed a pair of steals that sealed the victory.

Bird took over the second game, scoring 31 in Boston's 117-95 victory. "Larry had one of those special games of his," Walton said. "He was everywhere . . . his hands on every ball, stealing, passing, shooting, and rebounding. He did whatever he wanted to do." In Game 3 at Houston, the Rockets did what they wanted at the end. Down eight with 3:19 to play, they rallied to a 106-104 victory. It was survival of the roughest, Houston-style. "It was total chaos," said Bird of the Rocket rally. "It was like playing outside in the schoolyard."

The Celtics bounced back in Game 4 as Parish (22 points, 10 rebounds), McHale (19-9) and Walton (10-4 off the bench) battled the Twin Towers to a draw inside while Johnson (22) and Bird (21) gunned them down from outside in a 106-103 victory.

Tempers boiled over in Game 5 at Houston. Sampson was ejected early in the second quarter for hitting Johnson and Jerry Sichting. Still, the Rockets scored a 111-96 victory—despite a 33-point, 8-rebound effort from McHale—to force the series back to Boston.

Clearly, the Celtics were focused. The brawling had left both physical and emotional marks on K. C. Jones' team. "I had to call off practice," said the coach. "We were going after each other like Muhammad Ali and Joe Frazier. I'd never seen anything like that intensity in practice in all the time I've been here."

The Celtics carried their practice attitude over into the decisive sixth game. Boston dominated the Rockets from the opening tip as the Celtics rolled to a 114-97 victory and championship 16. Bird and McHale led the way with 29 points apiece. Among them, McHale, Bird, and Parish had 32 rebounds to 23 for the Twin Towers. Sampson all but disappeared in the game, scoring eight points on 4-for-12 shooting.

Bird was the word. For the second time in three seasons, Larry was the MVP of both the NBA regular season and the playoff finals.

"If you noticed Larry's jersey, you'd see five fingerprints on it," said K. C. Jones. "He carried us all the way." ♣

1986 locker room celebration champagne bottle

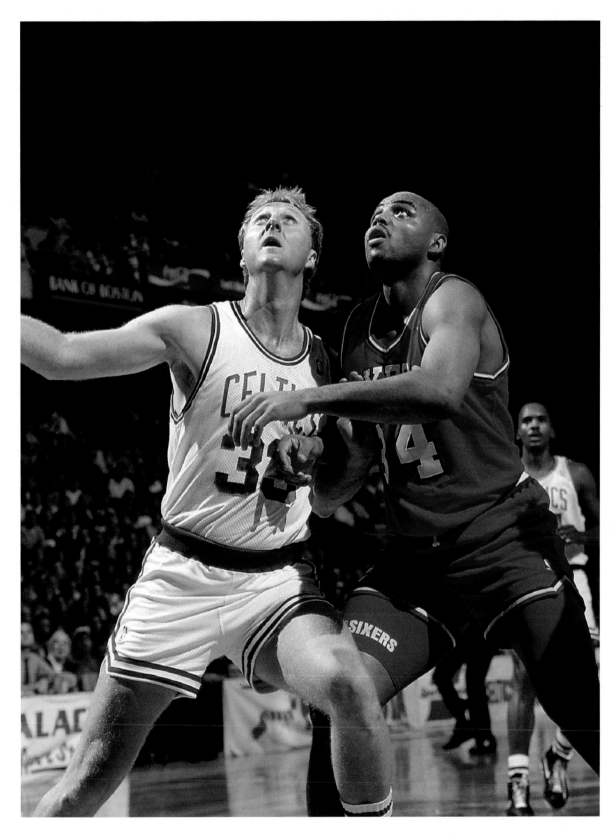

Larry Bird and Bill Walton are remembered as two of the most graceful players ever to play their positions in the NBA. And both were also adept at the physical side of the game as evidenced here. Pictured far left, Walton battles Laker center Kareem-Abdul Jabbar for rebounding position while Bird blocks out A. C. Green. Pictured here, Bird uses his body to fight for position against Charles Barkley of the 76ers.

FOLLOWING SPREAD:

Dennis Johnson pops the champagne in Boston's chaotic locker room as the Celtics celebrate their 1986 NBA Championship.

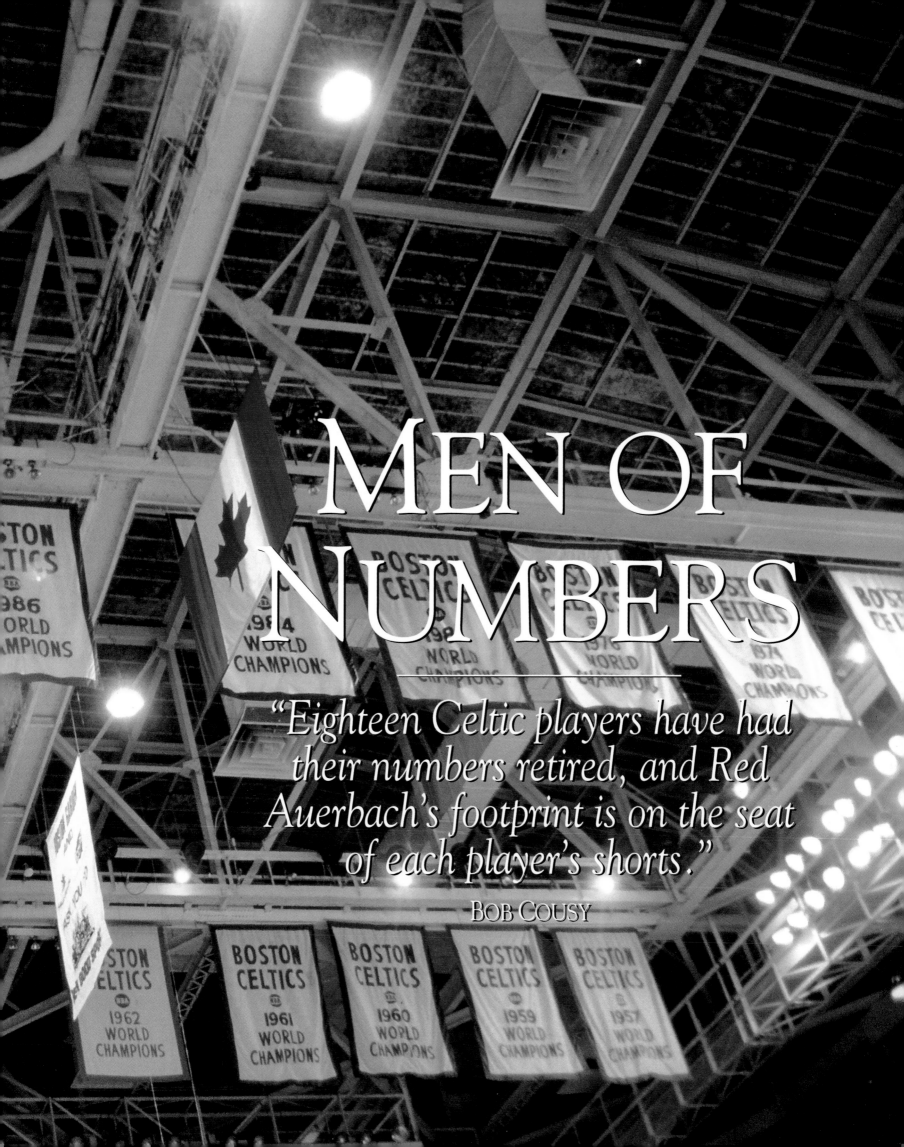

MEN OF NUMBERS

"Eighteen Celtic players have had their numbers retired, and Red Auerbach's footprint is on the seat of each player's shorts."

BOB COUSY

CELTICS GREATS

"No other basketball team has had the parade of winning players we've had. That's why all those numbers are stuck up on the ceiling."

RED AUERBACH

It is a galaxy unmatched in basketball. The Celtics would need a bus to transport all their Hall of Famers up the Massachusetts Turnpike to Springfield for a reunion. Of the 269 players who have worn Celtics Green, 17 now occupy pedestals there—with more on the threshold. (And that's not counting five nonplaying Celtics family members—Doggie Julian, Bill Mokray, and Honey Russell, and the two who created it all: Walter Brown and Red Auerbach.)

Admirers needn't travel 100 miles for a roll call of Celtics heroes, of course. A glance at the FleetCenter ceiling will do—scanning the numerals of 18 stars (plus Auerbach and Brown) retired above the parquet stage they dribbled across.

No other basketball team has had such a parade of talent. And Bob Cousy was the drum major.

Bob Cousy

"Bob Cousy *is* the Boston Celtics," Walter Brown used to say. "He was the most spectacular, inspiring, and greatest clutch performer I have ever seen in any sport. There will never be another Bob Cousy. Like Babe Ruth, he revolutionized a game. And like Babe Ruth, no one can ever take his place."

No one was in a better position than Brown to assess the Celtics' gifted number 14. Or his contribution. Cousy and Brown were two of the trio who saved the franchise when it flirted with financial collapse in the early fifties.

Brown nearly went broke keeping his Celtics alive. He hired Red Auerbach, the crafty architect who quickly recast the hapless team into an exciting winner if not yet champion. And Cousy was the electric on-court presence who not only was the engine that made the Green go, but the immensely popular attraction who—crucially—put customers in the Garden's seats and made them fans of the roundball game that was so strange to most Bostonians.

Had Cousy not done so, there would have been no Boston Celtics for Bill Russell to put over the top when he came to town in late 1956 and made a good team a great one. It was Cousy who kept the franchise alive with his crowd-pleasing magic that started the Celtics winning and turnstiles spinning, not only at the Garden but around the NBA as he helped establish the league.

It all nearly didn't happen, of course. Ironically, Auerbach and Brown originally had little interest in the prize rookie from Holy Cross. The Celtics needed a pivotman in that 1950 draft. And, like other NBA teams, the Celts were leery of Cousy's 6-foot-1 height and also feared that his fancy-Dan razzle-dazzle might not be effective in the pro game. But the Celtics were stuck with a savior after drawing the short straw in a special lottery. And in came young Cooz, skinny and gaunt, with long arms and big hands, and promptly became the Celts' first superstar.

Cousy had style and flair while coolly weaving his magic in a forest of tall men, proving there was a place in basketball for a normal-sized athlete. Fans marveled at his sleight-of-hand, oohing and aahing as he did things with a basketball that no one had seen before, a clever and flashy "Houdini of the Hardwood." Cooz was the picture-book ballhandler and playmaker as he quarterbacked the Celtics, controlling the ball as he ignited the fastbreak. He brought spectators out of their seats with his hypnotic dribbling (sometimes behind his back), bullseye passing (often looking one way, going the other), inventive playmaking, and clutch shooting. And he could play pressure defense, clutching and poking and stealing the ball.

Mostly, Cousy was *fun* to watch and he captivated Boston fans, who put him on a pedestal alongside the Red Sox's Ted Williams. Besides being thrilled by his dazzling talents, they loved that he was an ordinary-sized person competing against giants and frequently making them look silly—David and Goliath all over again.

Throughout New England, youngsters imitated Bob Cousy, and so did kids throughout the country as television began beaming NBA games nationally. He was the yardstick by which backcourt talent would be measured. As in "he's good, but he's no Cooz." Even The Fonz got into it, once asking pal Richie as they fiddled with a basketball on television's *Happy Days*, "Hey, who do you think you are, The Cooz?" All the while the accolades mounted as Cousy collaborated with sharp-shooting partners, first Bill Sharman, later Sam Jones, to give Boston basketball's best-balanced backcourt tandems.

En route to the Hall of Fame, Cooz was first team All-NBA 10 straight years, second team his last two seasons, the league's MVP in 1957, the Celtics' first. He played in the All-Star Game in each of his 13 seasons, was its MVP twice, and would be a landslide choice as the NBA's Player of the Decade for the fifties. But the distinction Cousy has always savored most is the six world titles earned by the Celtics during his seven seasons as captain from 1957–1963. Cousy now broadcasts the Celtics away games.

"Individual honors are nice," he says, "but basketball is a team game and championships are what it's all about."

I've always wanted to be the best. It wasn't enough to be very good. I had to be the best."
BOB COUSY

BOB COUSY

The only retired-number Celtic ever traded away in his prime, Easy Ed Macauley remembers coming back to the Garden to face his former teammates and fans. "It was a weird feeling," says Macauley, who returned wearing a St. Louis Hawks uniform, a team he later led as coach and general manager before the franchise moved to Atlanta. "But the fans treated me fine . . . usually, except one game I recall. The Boston-St. Louis rivalry had become rabid. We met in the finals two straight years—the Celtics winning in '57 and the Hawks in '58, remember? So one night the Garden crowd really got on us, including me. Well, that upset Walter Brown and he got on the public address system and told everyone to lay off Macauley because 'he's one of our own.' So the fans stopped booing us—and booed Walter! Walter was probably the greatest sportsman who ever lived and was much beloved. But nobody messes with Celtics fans, do they? Not even the man who invented the team. And right in his own building. I think God Himself would have problems if He walked in wearing an enemy uniform."

Ed Macauley

He wasn't called *Easy Ed* for nothing. Easy described Ed Macauley's graceful, satin-smooth style, especially his seemingly effortless sharpshooting, as in "easy does it" and "he makes everything look easy."

Easy was the look of most everything number 22 did on a basketball court as Macauley collaborated with Bob Cousy and Bill Sharman to be, as sportswriter Joe Fitzgerald once wrote, "sports' best-known triumvirate since Tinkers-to-Evers-to-Chance" of baseball legend.

With Red Auerbach's direction, the All-Star trio transformed the Celtics of the early fifties from feeble also-rans into solid contenders on the threshold of becoming champions—saving the franchise in the process.

It was the slender 6-foot-8 Macauley in the pivot, utilizing those quick hands to put up a variety of soft and deadly shots (including his slick hook, a Garden favorite) or zipping passes to Cousy and Sharman, the most dynamic backcourt of that decade and perhaps ever.

With speed and finesse along with that delicate scoring touch, Macauley was the best shooting and ball-handling center of that era, the hub of Boston's league-best scoring machine. He could hit from anywhere in the front court, including on the gallop as the trailer on the Celts' legendary fastbreak.

Easy Ed usually was among the NBA's top snipers in both points and accuracy. Four decades later, his 18.9-point scoring average for his six Boston seasons ranks third among all-

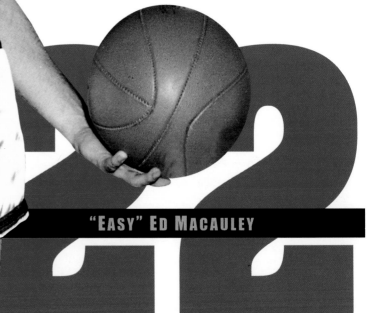

"EASY" ED MACAULEY

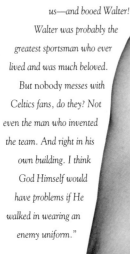

time Celtics, following Larry Bird's 24.3 and John Havlicek's 20.8.

It was Macauley, 1949's College Player of the Year with St. Louis University's powerful Billikens, who helped alter the image of centers from being considered overgrown freaks and goons. The Lakers' huge George Mikan was basketball's premier pivotman, but the smaller Macauley wasn't far behind. In fact, both were NBA first-team picks three straight years, 1951–53, Macauley's first three seasons in Boston after he was acquired when the St. Louis Bombers folded.

Macauley and Mikan waged resounding battles, including one memorable collision in 1953 when Easy Ed set the Garden's scoring record by pouring in 46 points over giant George. And in the first NBA All-Star Game, at Boston Garden in 1951, Macauley was MVP by scoring a game-high 20 points while holding Mikan to 12.

But more often Mikan's superior bulk, at least 60 pounds and three inches, wore down Macauley, who weighed closer to 180 than his listed 190. That was Macauley's shortcoming: lack of muscle against all the beefier centers, who hammered at him game after game. Easy Ed had brains, not brawn, and the deficiency meant a crucial shortage of rebounds.

"Ed had all the guts in the world, but he just wasn't big or strong enough against those horses," Auerbach says. "So he took an awful pounding."

Game after game, the beat went on. And over the long season, Macauley would be worn down by playoff time, and the Celtics eliminated early.

"I simply wasn't big enough physically to do the job on the boards," Macauley agrees. "I didn't have the muscle to compete with a Mikan and some others. No matter how I tried, and I busted my butt, I was not a good rebounder. And that's what the Celtics lacked, a big rebounder. Bill Russell would give them that, and how."

It was Macauley who enabled the Celtics to acquire rights to Russell, his successor, a player who would transform the Green into perennial champions. Walter Brown said he wouldn't make the trade unless number 22 agreed, and Easy Ed didn't stand in the way, a final major contribution to the Celtics.

Bill Sharman

Bill Sharman was the ultimate two-way guard, one of the best outside shooters of all time, and a relentless defender who hounded his man. For a decade Sharman teamed with Bob Cousy to give the Celtics basketball's best backcourt of the fifties, perhaps ever.

The Hall of Fame partners complemented each other, Cousy the flashy playmaker whose ballhandling magic created scoring chances and Sharman the sweet-shooting marksman who converted those opportunities into points. Individually they were extraordinary and even better together, and their slick collaborations electrified the Garden.

There were the Celtics galloping down the court on their patented fastbreak, Cousy leading the charge, then flipping the ball over his shoulder to the trailing Sharman, who would then nail a 20-foot jumper. Now there were the Celts weaving in the offensive zone as Cousy "fiddled and diddled" (according to Johnny Most) until someone broke free. And there was Sharman, always in motion, continually circling, eventually running his man into a jolting pick or into the floor to get open for a rifle pass from Cooz and an easy hoop.

"Willie would always get open," Cousy says. "Then his shot was automatic, the greatest shooter who's ever come along."

Number 21's picture-book shooting *was* deadly, both from the field and the free-throw line. He was one of the NBA's greatest all-time foul

CELTICSWEAR

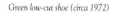

Black canvas low-top shoe (circa 1955)

White canvas high-top shoe (circa 1961)

Green low-cut shoe (circa 1972)

Black high-top shoe (circa 1986)

Black high-top shoe (circa 1996)

Celtic consistency includes fashions. The team has worn essentially the same simple-but-distinctive uniform design for nearly a half-century, ever since shedding its original colorful-but-passe costumes after the first year.

During that 1946–47 inaugural season the Celtics sported white T-shirts and shorts with green trim and lettering, a matching shamrock on each hip, white knee socks ringed by four green stripes at the top, black leather knee guards and high white canvas sneakers.

Warm-up suits were a shiny kelly sateen, featuring a white shamrock on the jacket's left chest.

The next season the team changed into conventional stirruped tops, while the shamrocked shorts and white high tops remained another year.

Except for improved fabric, there have been only minor changes in the Celts'

basic uniform over the decades, most noticeably length of shorts, which aren't short anymore.

Footwear has seen the biggest change in Celtics apparel. Boston was the last NBA team attired in canvas sneakers, wearing them through the sixties. By then most of the squad had long since switched from high- to low-top cuts. (Bob Cousy and Tom Sanders were among the last clinging to the high-tops.)

High or low, those black canvas beauties became part of the Celtics look, a trademark that was dictated not by design, as most assumed, but by practical and financial reasons, and by the porous parquet. During a game's constant pounding, dirt seeped up through the floor's many seams. "I figured black shoes wouldn't show the dirt," Red Auerbach explains. "Nothing looks worse than dirty sneakers. That's why we wore black ones."

In the seventies, the Celtics finally yielded to improved sneakers as basketball footwear became a big business. The Celtics' modern shoes were an appropriate green for years before adopting more fashionably correct black.

Fashionably correct was something one Celtic was not one day in the mid-fifties at Syracuse. Togo Palazzi arrived for the game against the Nats, but his equipment bag didn't. Undaunted, the former Holy Cross star borrowed orange road shorts from the Nats, turned an extra Celtics green road jersey inside out and inscribed it with his number 12, crudely made from adhesive tape.

"Togo," teammates remarked, "you look like a walking Italian flag."

Home uniform (circa 1976)

Away uniform (circa 1976)

Warm-up jacket (circa 1949)

Warm-up jacket (circa 1958)

Warm-up jacket (circa 1962)

Warm-up jacket (circa 1965)

Warm-up jacket (circa 1967)

Shooting shirt (circa 1968)

Warm-up jacket (circa 1976)

Warm-up jacket (circa 1986)

Trainers' jacket (circa 1995)

shooters with 88-percent accuracy during the regular season, 91 percent in the playoffs. Seven straight years Sharman led the league in free-throw percentage, including a record .932 in 1958–59. And he set the NBA record for consecutive free throws with 50, then topped it with 55, and outdid himself in the 1959 playoffs with 56 in a row.

Teammates considered Bill Sharman the league's best natural athlete, and he reflected that versatility by reaching the majors in two sports. Sharman had the distinction of being tossed out of a big league baseball game but never playing in one while riding the Brooklyn Dodgers' bench for a month as they blew the 1951 pennant. Bill was wearing Dodger Blue when New York Giant Bobby Thomson hit his dramatic playoff homer that sank the Dodgers. A week earlier, Sharman was ejected from a game when the umpire cleared the bench.

From the field, Sharman's 43 percent ranked him among the era's most accurate outside shooters and he played in eight All-Star Games (starting seven, including 1955 when he was MVP) and would be named to the NBA's Silver Anniversary Team. Four seasons in a row he was Boston's top point-getter, averaging nearly 21 points in a high-powered offense that spread scoring around.

"Not only was Bill a great, great pure shooter," Red Auerbach says, "but he was super on defense, the best I ever had in the backcourt until K. C. Jones came along."

Fueling those two-way skills were passionate competitive juices that boiled within the intense 6-foot-1 former USC All-American. Auerbach had pickpocketed his rights as a throw-in to a deal with the Pistons, who thought the Dodger prospect would stick with his first sports love, baseball.

Whatever the sport, the versatile Sharman was a Jekyll-Hyde. "Willie had two personalities," Cousy says of his nine-season roommate. "Off the court he was the most gentle and polite of men. When he put on that uniform something would happen and he'd switch into a killer mode."

"Bill had ferocious pride," Frank Ramsey adds. "He was the fiercest competitor of all."

BILL SHARMAN

Frank Ramsey

He was the Celtics' original "sixth man," a prototype who pioneered the role all the way to the Hall of Fame.

Although one of the NBA's better players, Frank Ramsey rarely started. Instead, the supersub swingman was perched on the bench waiting while Red Auerbach studied the game's tempo and decided when and where he could best utilize his versatile weapon.

Ramsey was equally gifted playing up front or in the backcourt, and could put a dagger into the opposition at either position. He had a knack of breaking open a game quickly, whether by nailing a jumper or drawing a foul—sometimes both at once.

So the heady "Kentucky Colonel" sat at the ready with his warm-up jacket open, so he could rip it off as he ran (never walked) to the scorer's table the instant the coach called his name—usually about six minutes into the game.

It was as though Auerbach were saying to the opposition, "So you think you have your hands full with Russell, Cousy, and our other starters. Well here comes Ramsey, baby. See what you can do with *him!*" It was like sticking in an ice pick.

And when Ramsey checked in his number 23, teammates and fans would guess how many ticks of the clock it would take until he scored. "Rams had a dramatic impact on any game within 15 seconds," Tom Heinsohn says. "Whether coming in upfront or in the backcourt, Frank made things happen. He was by far the greatest sixth man in basketball history."

Not starting didn't bother Ramsey. "I enjoyed that role and felt it was comparatively easy," says the former Kentucky All-American, who led the Wildcats to an NCAA title before coming to Boston in 1954 and contributing to seven championships in nine seasons.

"Even my size (6-foot-3 1/2, 190 pounds) had advantages. In the backcourt I was bigger than some opponents. And upfront I was faster than bigger forwards. And thanks to Russ, Heinie, Loscy, and Satch, I didn't have to worry much about rebounding. As soon as a shot went up, I could take off for the other end, and those bigger guys had to chase me. So I had some advantages as sixth man."

And some disadvantages, including that Ramsey never played in an All-Star Game. Even supersubs don't have the necessary stats. And there

Frank Ramsey played on seven NBA championship teams during his nine Celtics seasons, and the last title was the most emotional for him. Three decades later, Ramsey vividly recalls the Garden clock winding down as the Celts were defeating the Warriors in the 1964 finals to send the 34-year-old star back to his old Kentucky home a winner.

"Gee, it was tough," Frank says of that finale, when he contributed 18 points during his last 20 minutes on the parquet. "I looked up into the stands and everyone was cheering but one, my wife Jean. Tears were streaming down her cheeks. Probably mine too.

"The Celtics meant everything to us. I was proud every moment I wore that uniform. When people talk about great basketball teams, they generally agree the Celtics were the best of all. It was great to be a part of that, and it's something you can take to your grave."

After the game, Walter Kennedy squeezed through the locker room crowd and shook Ramsey's hand. "Frank," said the NBA commissioner, "you left just the way you came in, a star."

FRANK RAMSEY

was a rule restricting to three the number of players selected from one team.

"All that was a shame because Frank was truly a star," Auerbach says. "It was no fault of his that his ability wasn't fully recognized. He was an absolutely brilliant player who did anything and everything I asked of him. There was no better team player than Frank Ramsey. But in some ways that cost him."

Jim Loscutoff

It was Johnny Most who dubbed "Jungle Jim," and the nickname fit snugly. Jim Loscutoff looked like Charles Atlas in short pants. At 6-foot-5 and 235 pounds, he was built more like an NFL linebacker than an NBA forward. In his nine seasons as a Celtic he contributed his consider-

"JUNGLE JIM"   LOSCUTOFF

able brawn and basketball skills to seven world championship teams. In recognition, his "Loscy" banner now hangs alongside those title flags, the only Celt to have a nickname retired instead of numerals. His number 18 was kept active for Dave Cowens, who was still wearing it when Loscutoff was honored.

Loscy was a Boston favorite as a fierce competitor who did his team's dirty work as a no-nonsense enforcer, and his bruising exploits are etched in the memories of those who cheered him on gleefully.

There he was, springing for the bench and peeling off his sweatsuit, revealing a network of bulging muscles. A half-smile belied the fire in his eyes as he pranced to report into the game as the Garden surged with a special electricity. Red Auerbach needed punch in his lineup and was unleashing his pit bull, and the building began rocking in anticipation of the excitement almost sure to follow.

Jungle Jim Loscutoff impacted a game. Literally. When he checked in, something was bound to happen. Bodies likely would be bouncing off the parquet. Soon. You could see opponents almost wince when the horn sounded heralding Loscy's entrance. "Things just seemed to happen when I was around," Loscutoff smiles in recollection.

Nobody set a more immovable pick. Or a more set-in-concrete screen. Loscy boxed out staunchly and hit the boards with gusto, out-muscling bigger rebounders. And he put his rugged defense to good use while often shadowing the enemy's best-scoring forward. And most of all, never was there a more conscientious and intimidating basketball "cop" as he protected teammates from manhandling. Any foe reckless enough to strong-arm a Celtic had to answer to Loscutoff.

The legend of Jungle Jim Loscutoff has blurred appreciation of Loscy's hoop abilities. He was not Hulk Hogan on a basketball court; he knew what to do with a basketball.

Until the coming of Bill Russell, Loscutoff held the Celtics' single-game rebound record with 26 and was a starter for years until two career-threatening injuries took a toll. Boston's top draftee in 1955, out of the University of Oregon, bounced back from knee and disc operations, shifting to the off-the-bench enforcer role that was a vital ingredient in Auerbach's championship formula.

"Loscy was very underrated," says Red, who still bristles at any suggestion that Jim was just a brawling tough guy. "He was a much, much better player than generally given credit for. He could shoot and was fast for his size. But there's only one ball, and I already had people who could score. What I needed was someone to set picks and box out. Jim was great at that, but who ever writes about setting picks? That's not a glory job, but it's necessary, and Loscy did it, and never complained about not getting the headlines. And Loscy was very conscientious about keeping opponents in line. So he was considered an arch-villain around the league. Those fans considered him an animal and called him worse names than 'Jungle Jim.' But deep down, while screaming at him, they were wishing Loscy was on their team. If he had, they would have been cheering like hell for him."

Retired heavyweight boxing champion Rocky Marciano once suggested to Jim Loscutoff that he quit basketball for boxing and offered to be his manager.

"I told Rocky thanks but no thanks, that I had stomach trouble, no guts," Loscy laughs. "My face isn't much to look at, but I like what I've got."

Tom Heinsohn

Celtics teammates didn't call him "Tommy Gun" and "Ack-Ack" and "Gunner" for nothing. Tom Heinsohn loved to shoot a basketball.

He had a devastating arsenal of shots, featuring running line-drive hooks and no-arc jumpers. All had little or no trajectory, the result of learning to shoot in a low-ceilinged neighborhood gym. His marksmanship style gave new meaning to the term "straight shooting." And shoot Heinsohn did, all the way to the Hall of Fame. "Heinie lived for his next shot," writer Joe Looney once said. And Joe Fitzgerald has written, "Tommy never found a spot he couldn't shoot from."

"He'd throw up shots from anywhere," Celtics roommate Jim Loscutoff says. "When Tommy had a basketball in his hands, he had no conscience, none. At one All-Star Game, Dick Hemric and I were sitting in the stands and figured out that Heinie touched the ball 23 times and shot it 21. And the only reason he didn't shoot it the other two times was that once he got stuck with the ball at midcourt and had to dribble it around, and the other time he bounced the ball off his foot out of bounds. And that was in 1957, when Heinie was a *rookie*. When it came to shooting, Tommy was never bashful."

Nor was any other part of number 15's rugged game. The 6-foot-7 supercompetitor performed as a complete forward who was a heady student of basketball, a quality he would prove again as an NBA Coach of the Year.

"Tommy Heinsohn was a tough, gutty kid and an ideal forward," Red Auerbach says. "He was a clutch performer who could do it all: great offensive rebounding, great moves, great shots, including a beautiful soft hook, even great defense when he felt like playing it. And as Frank Ramsey used to say, Tommy would knock down his grandmother for two points. Heinsohn was a winner. Period."

A winner with 10 championships to prove it.

When the Holy Cross All-American arrived as the Celtics' 1956 territorial draftee, no green-and-white banners hung from the Garden rafters. When he retired nine seasons later, there were eight. Tom probably would be nine for nine if Bill Russell hadn't chipped that ankle bone in the 1958 finals. And Heinsohn would add two more championships as coach, coming out of retirement at dynasty's end to rebuild Celtics fortunes in the seventies.

Heinsohn's winning ways did not save him from being Auerbach's favorite whipping boy. Not only did the coach need a thick-skinned scapegoat to flog at halftime to stir more sensitive mates, but Red thought Heinie responded better to the lash while pushing to extract the maximum from his abilities.

Smarting, Heinsohn would come out roaring for the second half with something to prove: crashing the offensive boards with gusto . . . challenging foes (like Wilt Chamberlain, who broke a hand when, taking a punch at his tormentor, he smacked the back of his own teammate's head instead) . . . hands on hips and making rubber faces, snarling at opponents and referees. And most of all, shooting—racing down the court on a fastbreak, his right hand aloft, beckoning for the ball so he could greedily do his thing.

Shooting, that's the role the Celtics counted on Heinsohn filling despite all the ribbing. The team already had the league's premier defenders, Russell in the middle, Tom Sanders up front and K. C. Jones in the backcourt. What the Celtics needed was a sniper to consistently put the ball in the basket. "I wanted Tommy to shoot, that was his job," Auerbach says. "He was under my orders to shoot every time he had a good shot."

And Heinsohn did, and well, although, surrounded by the Celtics galaxy, never getting full credit as one of the NBA's premier forwards. He was a six-time All-Star whose 18.6-point average ranks fourth on the club's all-time list. "Tommy had the greatest variety of effective shots in the league," teammate Bill Sharman would admire, significant praise from one of the most scientific and consistent sharpshooters ever. "And he isn't afraid to use them."

TOM HEINSOHN

Tom Heinsohn played key roles in 10 Celtics championship campaigns— eight as a player and two (1973–74 and 1975–76) as coach. Heinsohn the player was a study in apparent contradictions . . . a physically rugged defender and rebounder who thrived on contact under the boards. On offense, however, Heinsohn possessed one of the sweetest, most accurate shots among the league's forwards.

Never, although those who never saw him play must wonder if Heinsohn's fondness for launching a basketball may be exaggerated by legend. "Let me put it this way," seven-season teammate Bob Cousy has said, setting the record straight about his close friend and broadcast partner. "Tommy never shot unless he had the ball."

Bill Russell

Bill Russell will forever be known as the player who changed basketball, the super superstar who introduced a new defensive style and dimension to the sport.

"Russell revolutionized basketball," Bob Cousy says. "He changed the patterns of play, both for individuals and teams. And first and foremost, Russ was a team man, the one who made us go. Without him we wouldn't have won a championship."

With him the Celtics compiled a never-to-be-matched necklace of 11 NBA diamonds during Russell's 13 seasons, and likely would have added a 12th championship if he hadn't gotten hurt during the 1958 finals.

From the day he donned number 6, Russell transformed the Celts from a good team to a great team when he joined them from the Melbourne Summer Olympics late in 1956. He was the final ingredient in Red Auerbach's dynasty recipe, the rebounder who could seize the basketball. And how.

"Russ was the guy we desperately needed," Auerbach says. "And he turned out to be everything I expected and more, the greatest of them all, the best basketball player who ever lived."

"There can be no doubt Bill was the key to all those championships," says Easy Ed Macauley, the star the Celtics dealt to the St. Louis Hawks for the rights to Russell after the prize center had led the United States to Olympic gold and the University of San Francisco to a 57-1 record while winning two NCAA championships.

"Cousy, Sharman, Heinsohn, the Joneses, and all the others were great players. But if you had taken any one of them away, the team still would have accomplished everything it did even though it would have been more difficult. But not if you had taken away Russell. Then it would have been impossible."

"There was only one Russell and we had him, thank goodness," Tom Sanders says. "That was the difference. In my lifetime no team in any sport has had such a dominant figure. I've never seen Russ' singular consistency in superior ability, effort, and drive duplicated. He thought, absolutely believed, that he could win every year. And he nearly did."

"There's nobody else like him," Alex Hannum has said, an admiring victim both as a player and coach. "He's in another world."

Almost literally, as Russell went ballistic in protecting the basket game after game, usually playing nearly the full 48 minutes. He utilized a kangaroo leap and octopus reach to harvest rebounds and block shots to unfurl the Celts' fastbreak, demoralizing and wearing out opponents while delighting Boston fans.

There was the 6-foot-10 Russell soaring to reject a shot, and in the same motion steering the ball to Cousy, who already was in gear setting the fastbreak in motion before the enemy could recover. And there was Russell springing to sweep the boards of a rebound, feeding an outlet pass to K. C. Jones to trigger another breakout. And Russell, parlaying extraordinary timing, quickness, and speed, did it with a grace and power befitting ballet.

Bill Russell's relationship with Red Auerbach was special and endured the test of time and the rigors of competition. In Russell, Auerbach saw not only a great player but a brilliant tactician and leader of men. After winning two championships in the exhausting dual role of player-coach, Russell retired. Russell was then voted the NBA's Player of the Decade for the sixties.

Many opponents used to tell
me they had nightmares about Bill Russell.
'God,' they'd say, 'I wake up in a sweat and see
this big black hand over me.'
And they were absolutely serious. Russ
had an entire league psyched as
he revolutionized basketball."

BOB COUSY

Russell the Intimidator sometimes prevented baskets even when not leaving his feet, or even being in the vicinity as gun-shy foes suffered from what opponent Tom Hawkins called "Russell-phobia." An opponent with a clear shot expected him to swoop down from nowhere, and worried, *where is he?*—and not infrequently blew the shot. All those missed points don't show among Russ' stack of defensive records.

"No one has ever played defense like Russell," fellow Hall of Famer Bob Pettit says of the four-time NBA MVP, chosen both the league's Player of the Sixties and All-Time Greatest Player in 1980.

No player was ever better in the clutch, or at his best in the biggest games when a rebound or blocked shot was crucial. All the while Russell was making teammates better in a variety of ways. They could gamble on a steal, confident he would cover for them. And when an opponent shot, they could get a headstart on the transition to offense and sprint upcourt, aware Russell rarely needed help on the boards. And Russ helped simply being the type of superstar he was.

"There are two kinds of superstars," Don Nelson once told Joe Fitzgerald. "One kind makes himself look good at the expense of the four other men on the floor. The other kind makes the four men around him look better than they are. That's the kind of superstar Bill Russell was. He made us all look better than we were."

The man knew how to win, and it rubbed off.

BILL RUSSELL

Sam Jones

"In the seventh game of a championship series," Bill Russell has said, "I'll take Sam Jones over anyone who ever stepped onto a basketball court. When the pressure was greatest, he was eager for the ball."

Russell said he always knew how his 12-season Celtic teammate would react in the huddle during the final seconds of a crucial game.

"Gimme the ball and get out of the way," Jones would say, according to Russ. "I'll make it." And, Russell said, "you knew he'd make it."

Sam usually did, coolly driving a stake into the enemy's heart as the final horn sounded. That was Sam Jones, the graceful Celtics sniper who thrilled Boston fans for more than a decade with his clutch marksmanship as the Celts' shooting guard.

He arrived in Boston in 1957 as a little-known number-one draft choice from tiny North Carolina College. And after a four-year apprenticeship behind Bill Sharman, he became one of the best shooting guards in basketball history as he teamed first with Bob Cousy and then with K. C. Jones in memorable tandems. Along the way he helped the Celtics collect 10 world championships to not only earn a berth on the NBA's 10-player Silver Anniversary Team, but a niche in the Hall of Fame.

Jones was nicknamed "Sudden Sam" and "Slippery Sam" (both by Johnny Most, of course) along with "Sad Sam," and all three fit: *Sudden* because of Sam's quickness and speed, *slippery* for his elusiveness and deception, *sad* because he looked that way with his woeful facial expression.

But there was nothing sad about Sam on a basketball court. At 6-foot-4, not quite 200 pounds, Jones was the prototype of the big guard that would become standard in the NBA. Sam utilized his size and strength advantages along with probably the league's fastest legs, speed ideally suited to the Celtics' fastbreak. As lean and swift as a greyhound, long-legged number 24 was always moving, and popping his assortment of picture-book shots.

Jones had a classic and deadly touch as

Red Auerbach was a storied disciplinarian, yet fined only one Celtic, Sam Jones. For eating pancakes. "That's right, pancakes," Sam says. "We played Syracuse on a Saturday night in Boston, and after the game flew to Syracuse for a return game Sunday," he recalls. "As soon as we landed, Russ, K. C., and I went looking for a place to eat. There was a team rule against eating pancakes, but we all ordered them anyway.

While the others were gabbing, I got my order first, so I took a bite and heard a voice yell, 'That will be five dollars!' I look around and who's standing there but Auerbach. So I say, OK, I might as well pay the fine and enjoy my meal. I dig for another forkful and Red says, 'Take another bite and it'll cost another five dollars.' Meanwhile, Russ and K. C. are yelling to the cook: 'Cancel those orders! Cancel those orders!'"

SAM JONES

he led Celtics scorers in accuracy season after season, armed with an arsenal featuring his nothing-but-net bullseyes pushed from the corner and his signature bank-shots that kissed the glass softly as Sam niftily played the backboard the way a slick pool player uses a cushion. And as Jones released his perimeter shots over the desperate flailing of a beaten defender, Sam would often call out, "Too late!" not so much taunting as expressing a matter of fact.

Sam's production was the result not only of dead-eye marksmanship (one or two-handed, it didn't matter), but also of his elusiveness in getting free to shoot. That included utilizing a superquick first step and a variety of out-of-your-jock fakes. "I've never seen anyone who can get himself into shooting position as fast as Sam," Frank Ramsey would marvel, calling Jones "the best shooter in the league." And Sam probably was as he set most of Boston's scoring marks of that era, including 49 points in a 1965 game before eclipsing that with 51 points two years later.

Through it all, number 24's Celtics role was simple. "Whenever the Celtics were nine points down," Pulitzer Prize–winner Jim Murray once wrote, "it was Sam Jones' job to tie the score." And when he did, Murray might have added, it would be to take one more shot, the buzzer-beater that won the game.

K. C. Jones

The sight of K. C. Jones stalking his man on the parquet always excited Celtics fans. There he was, picking up his opponent inbounding the ball at one end of the court and dogging him step-for-step all the way up the floor. You could almost hear K. C. yipping.

Number 25 played ferocious defense, pressing his man the length of the court—unless he stole the ball first, which often happened with his lightning timing and reflexes. And it wasn't just any foe that Jones was shadowing, with or without the ball. It was the enemy's best shooting guard: Jerry West or Oscar Robertson or Hal Greer. Game after game, K. C. played with dynamite.

Small at an even six feet, K. C. Jones tirelessly wore them all out: so quick, so strong, and so relentless as he pressured constantly. Stopping, starting, sneakers squeaking on the hardwood. Always in their faces, always pestering as he kept his opponents off-balance and gave them claustrophobia while tying them in knots.

K. C. JONES

"I loved playing alongside Case," Sam Jones says. "That meant I didn't have to play against him. I'd look at the poor souls he was haunting and was thankful it wasn't me. Thank you Lord, thank you."

Sam and K. C. were a pair of aces, the Celtics' backcourt admired around the NBA as "the Jones boys." Just when Celtics foes were sighing with relief to be rid of Bob Cousy and Bill Sharman as basketball's best backcourt, along came understudies Sam and K. C. to terrorize them. Opponents had difficulty keeping up with the Joneses, particularly with Sam's sharpshooting and K. C.'s ballhawking. And while Sam received the attention that goes with scoring, K. C. was shortchanged because defense wasn't as appreciated.

"K. C. never got the recognition he deserved," Red Auerbach says. "He was a fantastic player and just superb on defense."

The stingy guard was in good company, collaborating with center Bill Russell and forward Satch Sanders as basketball's best-ever defensive trio, envied by long-suffering Lakers coach Fred Schaus as "three of the greatest defensive players ever, all on the same team."

"Next to Russell, K. C. was the Celtics' most valuable player," Hall of Famer Jerry West used to say of his tormentor. "You can replace Sam with a Havlicek, and most of their forwards could be replaced by someone off Boston's bench. But nobody could do the things that K. C. does to me."

"K. C. was the best defensive man in basketball," Russell has said of the Celtics' No. 3 draft choice in 1956. He was the first NBA draftee ever selected solely on the merits of his defensive ability. Russell continued, "Over the years I saw him do superhuman things and make them look natural. He was a marvel, the best."

Russell should know. Incredibly, he and K. C. teamed in 11 title teams in succession: on back to back NCAA titlists at the University of San Francisco in 1955 and 1956, on the United States gold medalists at the 1956 Olympics and then, after Jones joined the Celtics after an army hitch and a brief fling with the NFL's Los Angeles Rams, on eight straight NBA champs.

Not even Russell collected rings his first eight Celtics seasons. Only K. C. has that distinction in hoop history to earn his place in the Hall of Fame, a career 7.4-point scorer. Admitted not for what he put into the basket but for what he kept out. And Jones wasn't through. After retiring as the team's crisp-passing quarterback (following Cousy's retirement) and defensive pillar, K. C. would return a generation later to earn three more rings, one as an assistant in 1981, and two more as he coached the 1984 and 1986 World Champion Celtics. So K. C. Jones, now back with the Celts as an assistant, was a vital part of 11 championship flags hanging from the rafters, and one number, 25.

Tom Sanders

He never made an NBA All-Star squad and his career scoring average wasn't in double figures. Yet his number 16 is fittingly retired with those of the Celtics' greats.

Tom "Satch" Sanders was the ultimate defensive forward who was overshadowed by a galaxy of star teammates who got most of the attention. Not being an All-Star didn't bother the 13-season Celtic. "That wasn't important. I had what a lot of All-Stars wanted but couldn't have, championships," says Sanders, a major contributor to eight Celtics crowns in a nine-year period.

*S*omeone has to do the dirty work. Tom "Satch" Sanders, shown here in his later coaching role, made a storied career out of doing all the little things that never show up in the scorebook—playing rugged defense, throwing screens, blocking taller rebounders off the boards, hustling for loose balls. In other cities, he might have gone unnoticed. Not in Boston. A work ethic was bred into Celtics fans. A member of 11 championship teams, he was also one of the favorite players with the fans.

That gave the former NYU All-American not only a ring for nearly every finger, but another important consolation. "Cashing the checks that went with them covered a lot, too," says Sanders, now an NBA vice president.

And there was something even more satisfying as Satch went about the thankless task of trying to shut down the enemy's best-scoring forward. "I had the satisfaction of walking back to our bench, where Red (Auerbach) and the guys knew I had done my job well," he says.

The soft-spoken 6-foot-6, 210-pounder, along with K. C. Jones, the quiet men and dry-wit humorists of that Celtics era, *did* have the respect of teammates. "Satch got hardly any recognition," says Tom Heinsohn, who played the opposite corner from Sanders and later coached him for four seasons. "But he did more to help our team than anyone realized. Except for his teammates. We knew."

So did the opposition. "When I think of Boston's great defense, I think of Satch Sanders,"says Hall of Famer Elgin Baylor, whose Lakers were frustrated seven years in the NBA finals by the Celtics. "He enjoyed playing defense. Satch was the toughest defender I ever went against, very aggressive but never dirty. And totally unselfish. And he was consistent every game."

Nine hundred and sixteen of them, still sixth most ever played by a Celtic, including 459 in a row, then the team's ironman record. Not bad for someone who didn't want to be a Celtic.

"I wasn't enthusiastic about being drafted by Boston," says Sanders, the Celts' top pick in the 1960 draft. "I was from New York City, so was a Knicks fan and had scrimmaged against them at NYU. I was hoping to play with them and stay in my hometown. Also, the Knicks had finished last the previous season and needed help. In contrast, the Celtics were basketball's best team, having won three championships in four years. Making their squad would be an uphill battle, top draft choice or not. I was also tempted by an offer from Tuck Tape to join its management training program and play for its AAU team. But Red went to work on me. He talked to me like a father. He said I could always get a job, but a chance to play pro ball comes along once in a lifetime, especially with the world champions. He also said Gene Conley was tiring of playing two big-league sports and that Jim Loscutoff's back was hurting, and kept stressing there was room for me. By the time Red finished with me I envisioned myself rushing to the rescue of the world champs. Then I got to training camp and found about 25 forwards fighting for *my* position."

16

TOM "SATCH" SANDERS

Auerbach did have a key role for Sanders. Defense was a crucial part of Red's championship mix. While other coaches focused on offense, Auerbach put at least equal emphasis on defense. And the Celts already had the greatest defensive center ever in Bill Russell and the most tenacious guard in K. C. Jones. Now Auerbach wanted an adhesive in-your-jock forward to hound the Baylors, Pettits, and Twymans.

Sanders had all the qualities: aggressiveness, quickness along with galloping speed, rugged inside strength, marvelous timing, and could leap. He was also a thinking man, one of seven Celtics who one day would coach the team. And vitally, Satch had the temperment, a selfless attitude. He believed in the team concept of being part of a winning machine.

"Once I got into the role I didn't miss scoring," Sanders says. "I took pride in what I was asked to do. I came to appreciate defense all the more, having so much fun going head-to-head against some of the greatest forwards of all time. It was a super challenge and very satisfying when you closed down those people, guys who could embarass you if you let them." That rarely happened, but Sanders paid a price in missed ovations and headlines.

"Winning is what counts, not the personal glories," he says. "The important thing was being able to say I was part of the world champion Celtics, and to know I had contributed."

John Havlicek

"John Havlicek," Red Auerbach has often said, "is what being a Celtic is all about."

Number 17 *was* the consummate Celtic, the epitome of excellence, selflessness, hustle, and the Celtics way.

He was immortalized for swiping a basketball—"Havlicek stole the ball!"—but that was just one among a treasury of heroics during 16 memorable seasons as the NBA's best two-position player ever.

John Havlicek wasn't defined so much by statistics, even though he played the most games, clocked the most minutes, and scored the most points (while dishing out the second-most assists) in team history. What's significant is how Hondo did it all while providing the glue that connected the Russell and Cowens eras to collect eight championship rings and a Hall of Fame pedestal.

He was the quintessential hustler, at full throttle from opening tap to final horn no matter what the score, the tireless Celt who never stopped running

Red Auerbach put almost as large a premium on athletic ability as basketball ability. So John Havlicek was the perfect Auerbach player. Versatile enough to be signed by the Cleveland Browns despite never playing college football, "Hondo" became the Celtics' "sixth man." Havlicek provided instant offense and defense, both as a "sixth man" and later as a starter, a star in both roles.

JOHN HAVLICEK

while leaving opponents gasping.

And he was the ultimate competitor. "God, what a competitor," Hal Greer has admired, the same 76er star from whom Havlicek burgularized a basketball to create the most celebrated moment in Celtics lore.

Havlicek could beat you in a variety of ways, and did. Starting or off the bench. At forward or guard. On offense and defense. Perpetually in motion with or without the ball as he ran opponents ragged with legendary stamina and consistency. And he did it in the clutch. As Clif Keane once wrote: "Two headlines you'll never see are 'Pope Elopes' and 'Havlicek Chokes.'" And Ray Fitzgerald once wrote: "Havlicek was the one you looked to for the tying basket at the buzzer, for the dramatic steal of a pass, for the play that would ignite a comeback."

It was all this, and more, that made Havlicek one of America's most admired athletes. Bill Russell was among enthusiasts. "If I were playing in an imaginary pickup game among all the players I've ever seen, he's the one I would choose," Russell mused in his book, *Second Wind.*

Significantly, it was Russell who picked Havlicek, a 26-year-old nonstarter, to succeed him as captain when Russ became player-coach, thus tapping another Hondo quality, leadership. Havlicek would fill that role a dozen seasons across two eras until he retired.

From the day in 1962 that the 6-foot-5 crewcut All-American from Ohio State reported as Boston's top draftee to the day he played his then-NBA-record 1,270th game in 1978, Havlicek not only fit the Celtic mold but was its poster boy. He did it all, including leading the team in points 10 times, nine seasons in a row, and leading in assists six years, while a perennial fixture on the league's all-defensive team.

He was named All-NBA 11 times (four first-team, seven second-team), and no Celtic has played in more All-Star Games, 13. In 1980, he was selected to the league's 11-player 35th anniversary team.

It's stuff legends are made of, and this one is all true. Well, almost. One part is a bit of a myth: the suggestions that Havlicek was literally tireless. "I tried not to let myself think about getting tired," Havlicek says. "If I felt a little tired, I figured the other guy must feel the same way, too. So I kept pushing."

All the way to Springfield.

Don Nelson

He was Red Auerbach's biggest steal, the Celtics' best bargain ever.

Don Nelson's number 19 got up to the ceiling the hard way. Of all the retired Celtic numerals, his is the only honoring a retread, a discarded free agent plucked from the NBA scrap pile. The salvaging of Nelson was another testament to the shrewdness of Auerbach, who saw something in the unemployed forward that no one else did as every league team waived on the obscure castoff.

Whatever it was, the crafty Nelson stuck around with the Celtics for 11 seasons and five world titles, along with John Havlicek spanning the Russell and Cowens championship eras of the sixties and seventies.

"Don Nelson," Bill Russell has said with admiration for Nellie's struggle to success, "epitomizes what it meant to be a Celtic."

Nelson's struggle began at the start of the 1965–66 season when, after riding NBA benches for three years, he was cut by the Lakers who felt he didn't have enough natural ability. The 6-foot-6, 210-pound former Iowa star went unclaimed and thought his playing career was over at age 25.

FOLLOWING SPREAD:

The tradition—and parquet floor—moved before the 1995–96 season from Boston Garden, left, to the new, 18,624-seat FleetCenter pictured on the right.

Although it was an aging building rife with problems, many partisans loved the Garden's cozy atmosphere. Of the Garden, Red Auerbach said, "The place is alive with personality."

The FleetCenter carries Celtics tradition—the parquet, the banners, the heritage—forward into one of the most modern facilities in the NBA.

*I*t was the luckiest shot in basketball history," Don Nelson smiles, "but it counted."

It was one of the biggest field goals in Celtics history, certainly the most important and best-remembered in Nelson's career. It was a dramatic clutch basket late in Game 7 of the 1969 NBA finals at Los Angeles, a 108-106 thriller which gave the Celtics another championship. Their lead melted to a single point with about 80 seconds remaining, the Celtics mishandled the ball to the right of the key as the 24-second clock was about to expire. "I picked up the loose ball and rushed a 15-footer to at least put up a shot and beat the clock," Nelson recalls. "The shot didn't 'feel' good and I didn't think it would go in. I was just hoping it would hit the rim in time and give us a chance at a rebound." The high, arching shot banged against the back of the rim and bounced two or three feet straight up—then dropped through. Shwish! "I knew I had it all the way," the laughing Nelson assured teammates in the locker room celebration. "Of course."

"When you clear waivers, you're usually all done," Nelson says. "So I was stunned when Red called and invited me to Boston, especially since there were other forwards available who had better statistics. I was scared to death when I reported. I had to beat out Ronnie Watts, and Red had us battling head to head for days. When I got the contract I was sitting on top of the world. In less than a week I'd gone from the pits to the heights, from down and out to a job with basketball's greatest team."

Nelson would become part of that Celtics legend, achieving it with determination and intelligence, a model of offensive and defensive consistency, whether starting or off the bench. No Celtic ever got more out of his skills. Ask his old coaches and teammates.

"Don was a thinking man's player," Auerbach says of his star pupil, who at age 36 became an NBA coach for 19 seasons, three times collecting the Coach of the Year trophy named for Auerbach, who "changed my life."

"Nellie used what God gave him better than any basketball player I've ever seen," Paul Silas says.

"Nelson was a basketball freak," Tom Heinsohn says. "He couldn't jump. He couldn't run. He just made monkeys out of opponents by making their strengths work against them. He out-thought them."

"Nobody thought the way Nellie did," Havlicek says. "I never played with anyone who got as much out of his ability. He's number one."

"He was all head," Paul Westphal says. "And that's how he played basketball, with his head instead of his legs."

"I always had a problem," Nelson says. "I didn't have the size, speed, or jumping ability most forwards have, so I had to compensate by working at it and trying to play a smart game instead of an emotional one."

DON NELSON

For a competitor who had to battle, Nelson looked like one playing without strain. An outstanding shooter who rarely took a bad shot, he seemed effortless, whether hitting his dead-eye medium-range jumper or driving opponents mad underneath with his YMCA up-fake that tickled Garden fans. Or flipping his patented one-hand free throws. And Nelson was a player to go at crunch time, a battler who knew all the tricks and a cool sharpshooter who delivered in the clutch while quietly collecting 12,475 career points, including playoffs.

"Because his style was so deceptive and unspectacular, Nellie's contribution over the years went largely unnoticed," Havlicek says. "But we knew and so did our opponents."

Jo Jo White

He was silky smooth, the durable gazelle with a stylish proficiency for deadly jumpshots and pinpoint passes.

Jo Jo White was the Celtics ironman who rolled gracefully through 488 consecutive games, still the team record, during 10 memorable seasons in Boston. He was the dual presence as a fluid marksman/playmaker, the backcourt ignition for the Celtics' five straight division titles and two world championships during the seventies.

His career almost over before he got to Boston, Don Nelson found his niche with the Celtics. "I started learning basketball the day I arrived in Boston," Nelson said years later. "From Red on down, the Celtics had a special way. He demanded, but he also taught. Everything you did was about being a Celtic. Winning was important, but winning in the Celtics tradition was more important. No shortcuts, just hard work."

Number 10 was the epitome of cool, equally placid taking a clutch shot or powering the fast break at crunch time. He made it all look easy, even when icily contributing 33 pressure points during a 60-minute masterpiece that spelled triple-overtime victory over Phoenix, heroics that not only made White the 1976 playoff MVP but vaulted the Celtics toward their 13th NBA crown.

"Jo Jo White was a complete basketball player," says Tom Heinsohn, who coached him. "He ran the offense, called the plays, pushed the ball up the floor on the break, scored, and played the good defense. You couldn't ask for more than that. Jo Jo was a superstar."

Joseph Henry White arrived in Boston just as Bill Russell and Sam Jones left in 1969, ending the dynasty. The 6-foot-3 Kansas All-American was drafted No. 1 to replace Sam—huge sneakers to fill. And after reporting during the season from military duty, White was asked to do it immediately. "Never had any Celtic been thrown into a pressure cooker so early in his career and responded so effectively," Heinsohn says. "This kid was thrown to the wolves in midseason and did the job from the start." Once Jo Jo adjusted from Kansas' slow possession offense to Boston's fast-break, he joined John Havlicek and Dave Cowens as the vital Big Three components of the Celtics' rebuilding.

Cowens tended to matters in and around the pivot, Havlicek operated out of the corners and White throttled the fastbreak, poised and stonefaced as he guided the ball upcourt, eyes darting as he glided up the parquet looking for an open mate. Or take aim himself, a pure shooter and consistent scorer, whether sniping from the fringe or connecting off a drive.

They were a distinguished troika, although White was somewhat overshadowed by his partners. They were more animated while White seemed an effortless machine. And after games, Jo Jo rarely was the center of media attention. The press usually flocked to Havlicek, the seasoned captain who had provided a harvest of quotes for more than a decade. And the blunt and volatile Cowens was often good for something outspoken. By the time reporters got to the soft-spoken White's locker (if they arrived at all) there was little room left in their notebooks as deadlines beckoned.

So White got less ink than he deserved, and less appreciation of skills that made him a seven-time All-Star Game participant. He still ranks among the Celtics' all-time top 10 in a variety of categories. Bob Cousy is the only backcourtman with a higher scoring average than White's 18.3 (21.5 in the playoffs).

The lack of attention grated on White, but that rarely showed as Jo Jo went about being the quarterback who anchored two memorable Celtics backcourts five years in tandem with Don Chaney before being reunited with 1968 Olympic teammate Charlie Scott.

The performance of each dynamic duo resulted in a Celtics flag. But after the second one in 1976, when White collected that playoff MVP trophy, it was downhill for Jo Jo. The next season he was hobbled by a heel bonespur that would haunt him during his last Boston seasons and finally require surgery. And then there was a contract dispute.

White asked to be traded and was accommodated, packed off to Golden State. It was a move that White calls "one of the biggest disappointments of my life, even though I asked to be traded with mixed emotions. It had been a couple of bad years for me and I was discouraged and very frustrated. But it was still a jolt."

Yet it soon led to one of Jo Jo's golden Garden moments, when he returned wearing a blue uniform. Feeling "really strange" as he stepped onto the parquet for the first time as a foe, the building rocked with a standing ovation that "meant a lot to me."

A greater moment lay ahead, the ultimate Celtics tribute. Three Aprils later, standing on nearly the same spot, Jo Jo White saw his number hoisted to the Garden rafters.

JO JO WHITE

Dave Cowens

Dave Cowens played every game as though it were his last, someone once said.

The second most celebrated Redhead in Celtics history was the ultimate competitor, exuding enormous energy and will to win. Like a bubbling volcano, he burned with a passionate energy, a fierce combatant who revolutionized his position, shattering the mold of towering pivotman.

In a league that favored seven-footers, Boston's 6-foot-8½, 230-pound David battled Goliaths game after game, season after season—Wilt and Kareem, Thurmond and Reed, Lanier and Moses. No matter how much bigger, nobody pushed Cowens around during his 10 rarely dull Celtics seasons in the seventies. He made the big guys play his game, then wore them out. He proved there was a place for a smaller center in the land of the giants.

Instead of rooting himself under the offensive basket like the others, Cowens frequently roamed outside. From his extended shooting area, he could hit a turnaround jumper or left-handed hook; if trailed, he could zip a pass to a mate cutting through the paint just vacated. And on defense, Big Red continually wrestled his man, harassing him, shoving him off his shooting sweetspot, disrupting his game. And after muscling a rebound, often ripping the ball away from bigger boardmen, Cowens could ignite the fastbreak with a jump-pass downcourt for a 3-on-2, which he'd make 4-on-2 by galloping down the floor, sometimes taking a return pass for a layup. And the Garden would thunder approval, marveling at the hustler who had both started and finished the break—like a quarterback tossing a touchdown pass to himself.

It went like that the full 48, Cowens unleashing that energy at the opening tap and never stopping playing both ends of the court, all-out until the final buzzer. Seven-footers weren't used to that kind of game from a rival center, who compensated for a height disadvantage with speed and quickness, agility and stamina, and that smoldering emotion.

"Dave might have been the most emotional Celtic of all," Red Auerbach has said. "He played with incredible intensity. There was only one gear to Cowens' game: full speed ahead."

"Cowens approached the game the way Marines approach a war," Joe Fitzgerald once wrote.

Every game *was* a war for Cowens. He was as aggressive as a linebacker, and threw his muscle around like one. With raw strength he blocked shots, crashed the boards, planted resounding picks, and skidded headlong across the parquet diving for loose basketballs.

That relentless and reckless abandon seemed to invite injuries, but Cowens dismissed the suggestion. "I don't worry about injuries," he explained. "I don't get hurt because I'm the one doing the hitting. I'm the one going a little nutty out there."

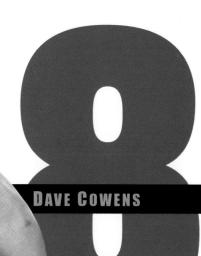

18
DAVE COWENS

"No Garden floorboard escaped a Cowens kneebone," Ray Fitzgerald once wrote. "To watch him dive after a loose ball was to see fury unleashed. No front-row patron was safe from Cowens' hurtling body, and even those rows farther back had best hang on to their hats."

"Dave didn't just play the game, he attacked it. And while doing that he became one of the greatest competitors of all time."
RED AUERBACH

arry Bird and Red Auerbach here at the beginning and end of one of the greatest runs in Celtics history. The Bird (above) was fresh out of Indiana State University and the club's No. 1 draft choice in 1978. The Bird (below) had just announced his retirement following the 1991–92 season. In between Larry led the Celtics to three NBA titles. He was the NBA's MVP three consecutive seasons (1983–84, '84–85, and '85–86) plus MVP of the '84 and '86 playoff finals. He was voted a first-team, All-NBA berth nine straight seasons.

Whatever it was, Dave Cowens provided the pivotal building block of the seventies Celtics. The top 1970 draftee out of Florida State proved the crucial middle man the Celtics desperately needed to win again. While proving wrong those who claimed he was too small, Cowens was a dynamic key to coach Tom Heinsohn's exciting renaissance team that had rekindled fan interest while winning five consecutive division titles and two world championships.

"Havlicek was the soul," Knicks coach Red Holzman noted; "Cowens was the heart."

That heart was a winner, the ideal Celtic—a team player who cared little for individual honors and stats while attracting them in abundance anyway. He's one of only four Celtics ever selected the league's MVP. He was all-NBA second team three times (somehow second team even when voted MVP in 1973), and three times all-defense. He played in seven consecutive All-Star Games, once the MVP. Year after year he led the Celtics in rebounding, three times in scoring and one season forged a triple—topping the team in rebounding, scoring, and assists. Averaging 18.2 points and 14 rebounds, he ranks among the top 10 in a variety of all-time Celtics categories.

Finally the years of intensity and pounding took their toll. Cowens' fires ebbed for awhile, and he took a sabbatical that lasted 30 games early in the 1976–77 season. His batteries recharged, Dave returned for three and a half seasons more, captaining the team and even coaching it most of 1978–79, joining Bill Russell as one of the Celts' only player-coaches. His passion could be restoked, but not a protesting body, and Cowens stunned basketball by abruptly retiring before the 1980 opener—worn out before his 32nd birthday.

And when they tacked the Hall of Famer's number 18 to the rafters, Red Auerbach glanced up and nodded: "No one ever played to win more than that guy. *No one.*"

Larry Bird

No one ever talks about where Larry Bird ranks on the Celtics' all-time scoring list (2), rebound list (4), or assist list (3).

No one even talks about how many championship rings he earned (3).

He's not an all-time NBA leader in anything, with the possible exception of quotable one-liners. The dossier is impressive enough (three-time MVP, nine-time first-team All-League, etc.), but others require more lineage. Awards, achievements, and stats do not define Larry Bird.

What they talk about is his aura. When you watched Larry Bird play the game, you quickly understood that if there was one person on earth who somehow personified all that was good about the game and who somehow encapsulated all the game had to offer, it was Larry Bird.

Opponents knew it. "Sometimes I wonder if the Celtic players fully appreciate his game," then-Knicks coach Hubie Brown said in 1985. "He's so great because he elevates everyone to his level."

His own coach knew it. "What comes to mind are the little things, " K. C. Jones once said. "It was the passion that made him dive over halfcourt to prevent a backcourt violation, and passion that made him knock heads diving for a loose ball. You'd see him go up for a rebound, and Larry can't jump, right? Then how come he always ended up with the ball? All those little things add up to greatness."

Erudite observers of the American scene most definitely knew it. "We live in an age of hype," declared author David Halberstam. "But in Larry's case, the reverse was true. It took a long time for the hype to catch up with the reality of how good he was."

And how good he was is almost impossible to describe. Just consider that he was good enough as a rookie to be first-team All-NBA, and that he then improved annually for at least the next six years. He had an inner voice which told him that he was never good enough, that if he didn't continue to work hard, someone would come along who might turn out to be better. No one ever had to tell Larry Bird to work on his game.

The strangest and most underappreciated aspect of the Bird legend is that he had an NBA career at all. For the physical entity known as Larry Bird who entered the NBA as a rookie in 1979 was not the same physical entity who had been Player of the Year at Indiana State a few months earlier. In the spring of that year Larry broke his right index finger in a bizarre softball accident. He was playing left field and he got his bare hand into the glove a bit too fast while catching a liner off the bat of his brother Mike. As team physician Dr. Thomas Silva would later explain, "There are breaks which are like snapping a pencil. Those are easy to fix. And there are breaks which are like someone smashing the finger with a hammer. Those are not easy to fix. Larry had that kind of break."

He therefore came into the league with the most important finger on his shooting hand a swollen, bent, ugly, and impaired unit. He had to redo his shot from scratch. It is hardly an exaggeration to suggest that many a player would have been defeated right there. Not Larry Bird. His whole career is a testament to the concept of mind over matter.

The Celtics knew they had something good in Larry Bird when they drafted him, but not even Red Auerbach knew how good. "What I didn't know about was his self-motivation," Red said, "and his willingness to pay the price by working hard. The more you paid him, the harder he worked. He wanted to show he was worth it."

Worth it? From a teammate standpoint, from a coaching standpoint, and from a fan standpoint, Larry Bird was always worth it.

When he retired after the 1991–92 season, he took it all with him. There was nothing for him to teach that wasn't observable to the naked eye. The rest is what made him Larry Bird.

"There's a secret to playin' basketball," he once said. "But I ain't tellin' what it is."

LARRY BIRD'S PROFILE BY BOB RYAN

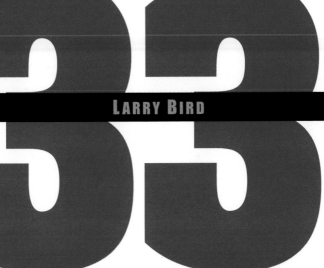

The crowning achievement. Larry Bird holds the 1986 NBA trophy over his head during public ceremonies celebrating the Celtics' championship.

FOLLOWING SPREAD

Larry Bird and Kevin McHale are poised for action as Robert Parish goes up for the game-opening tip against Kareem Abdul-Jabbar in one of the many Celtics-Lakers classics that highlighted the "Bird era."

LARRY BIRD

Kevin McHale

Kevin McHale was the Other Forward on basketball's best frontline ever.

He teamed with Larry Bird and Robert Parish in the eighties Celtics' dominating frontcourt partnership. It was an awesome threesome and powered the team to nine division titles and three league championships during a dozen years together.

McHale was overshadowed by the gifted Bird in the opposite corner, but forged his own imprint on basketball. While collaborating inside with Parish as "twin towers," McHale became master of the low post—the premier power forward of all time. He was the ultimate insider.

A gangling 6-foot-10 officially (probably closer to 6-foot-11), with squared shoulders and extra-long arms, McHale looked like Herman Munster, some joked. But the only thing Frankensteinesque about McHale was his monster game inside.

There was big number 32, posting up, his back to the basket, shuffling and wriggling as he muscled for elbow room. And there he was, faking free and digging into his arsenal of soft shots— jumphooks and turnaround jumpers, finger-rolls and scoop-ins, as he utilized remarkable timing and that boardinghouse reach to stretch over and around defenders. McHale's sharpshooting was accurate inside 18 feet, almost unstoppable inside 12.

"There isn't anybody in the league who can stop Kevin," Bird would say. "He can score on *anyone*. Even with two or three guys on him, he's going to score. And he makes it all look so easy."

And it wasn't only McHale's shooting, not just his career 17.9-point scoring and 55-percent marksmanship. Kevin was a versatile rebounder and shotblocker who played both ends of the court, utilizing the same coordination and mobility as a staunch defender as he did while proving a big man could dribble, pass, and run with the fastbreak.

"Kevin is the total package," Bird said. "He does it all: rebounds, blocks shots, runs the break—and is an absolute killer inside. He's the best in the world at what he does. Game in and game out, there's nobody who can do the things Kevin does." That consistency was a McHale hallmark. "You always knew what you were going to get from Kevin, and you could depend on it," says M. L. Carr, who teamed five seasons with McHale. "There were times when Larry was off and times when Robert was off, but few nights when Kevin was off. And if he was, that meant he'd shoot *only* 48 percent instead of 58 percent."

McHale was also the team comedian, a free spirit that sportswriter Jackie MacMullen called the Celtics' *Fun Master*. "Kevin loved to joke and fool around," said K. C. Jones, who coached him five seasons. "But when it came to basketball, he ceased being funny." And never more than at crunch time. "When the game's on the line," Bird said, "Kevin was ready—*always*."

Never was there a day when I didn't look forward to going out on the parquet and being a Celtic. It's an honor that remains with you long after your playing days are over. Like forever."

KEVIN MCHALE

KEVIN MCHALE

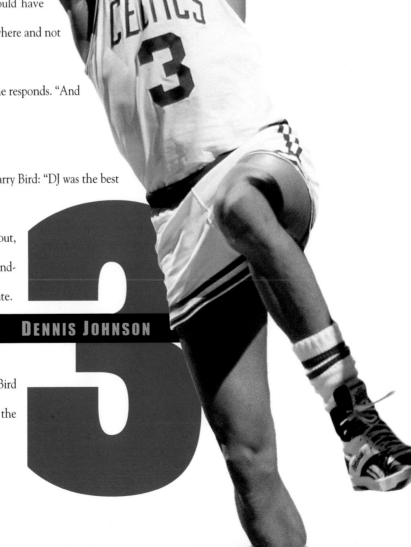

DENNIS JOHNSON

The 1982–83 Celtics had Bird, McHale, and Parish—but no title. Enter guard Dennis Johnson who arrived via trade and provided a backcourt ingredient that helped produce two championships in three seasons. DJ was a charasmatic leader, a leadership Red Auerbach cites as "a major reason for our success in the eighties."

A center-forward, the top 1980 draftee out of the University of Minnesota proved ideal for the sixth-man assignment, able to play anywhere upfront. He continued in that role four and a half seasons before succeeding Cedric Maxwell as a starter. The NBA's annual Sixth Man promptly became all-league—McHale and Bird both first-team forward choices as Kevin became the first NBA marksman to bullseye 60 percent from the floor, 80 percent from the line. He would play in seven All-Star Games and be named all-defense six times.

One of McHale's more memorable games occurred at the Garden on a Sunday afternoon in March 1985, when he scored a team-record 56 points, a mark broken nine days later when a teammate poured in 60—Bird, of course. But McHale held onto one record. Proving his 56 was no accident, Kevin added 42 in his next game—giving him 98 for both, the most by a Celtic in consecutive games.

By the time McHale's 13-season career ended in 1993—"it's been a great time, a great ride," he farewelled—Kevin had rung up numbers that rank him among all-time Celtics leaders in a variety of categories. Only Havlicek and Parish have played more games; only Havlicek, Bird, and Parish scored more points.

The question lingers of how much greater Kevin McHale's numbers would have been—and how much more attention he would have attracted—had he played elsewhere and not been second banana to Larry Bird.

"Yes, I would have scored a lot more points—and won a lot fewer games," he responds. "And it wouldn't have been nearly as much fun."

Dennis Johnson

Dennis Johnson will forever wear the mark stamped indelibly on him by Larry Bird: "DJ was the best player I ever played with."

The backcourt sparkplug was Bird's idea of what being a Celtic was all about, and the pair became soulmates who intuitively sensed each other's moves as they blended with rare chemistry. It was a dynamic duo that didn't need words to communicate. When the Celtics needed a big hoop, it was Johnson who generally got the ball to Bird, somehow penetrating a defense that knew what was coming.

Yet, with some poetic justice, there was a golden Celtics moment when Bird fed Johnson for a game-winning basket to climax a playoff thriller—again linking the two names in one of the NBA's most electric finishes ever.

The memory is frozen in Celtics history: May 26, 1987. The Eastern Finals are tied 2-2 in pivotal Game 5. With five ticks left on the Garden clock, Detroit has a one-point lead and the ball out of bounds at the Celtics' end of the court. That's when Bird rips off Isiah Thomas' inbounds lob and flips a pass over his shoulder to Johnson—hitting DJ in midstride as he dashes down the lane for the winning layup as the Garden erupts.

Yes, it was Bird who heroically stole the ball and made it all possible. But it was Johnson who instinctively cut for the basket, held off a swiping defender, and *made* the shot. It was the most remarkable moment in the memorable Boston career of the savvy quarterback of the Celtics powerhouses that succeeded to the NBA finals four times in five years in the mid-eighties—winning it all twice.

DJ was a winner from the time he arrived in 1983, plucked from Phoenix in a Red Auerbach/ Jan Volk trading heist. The 6-foot-4

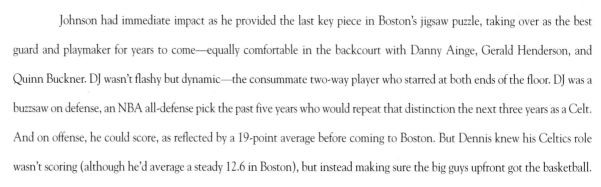

Pepperdine product brought along hard-nosed toughness and veteran's cool—and steadying consistency in the backcourt.

Johnson had immediate impact as he provided the last key piece in Boston's jigsaw puzzle, taking over as the best guard and playmaker for years to come—equally comfortable in the backcourt with Danny Ainge, Gerald Henderson, and Quinn Buckner. DJ wasn't flashy but dynamic—the consummate two-way player who starred at both ends of the floor. DJ was a buzzsaw on defense, an NBA all-defense pick the past five years who would repeat that distinction the next three years as a Celt. And on offense, he could score, as reflected by a 19-point average before coming to Boston. But Dennis knew his Celtics role wasn't scoring (although he'd average a steady 12.6 in Boston), but instead making sure the big guys upfront got the basketball.

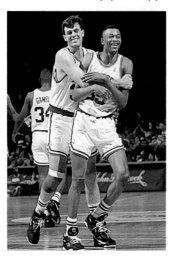

Reggie Lewis had matured into an NBA All-Star and the team captain prior to his tragic death in 1993. "Reggie had a great love for basketball," Red Auerbach said. "He played it with joy."

DJ was a clutch performer who thrived on big games, big plays, big moments—never better than during the playoffs, when championships were on the line. And it rubbed off. "Dennis made everyone on the team more effective—including the coach," says K. C. Jones, who coached the Celts during Johnson's first five seasons. "He was like having another coach on the floor."

Johnson had arrived with one diamond ring from Seattle's 1979 champions and added two more with the 1984 and 1986 Celtics. Now he hungers for more—in his fourth season in a new Celtics role: assistant coach.

Reggie Lewis

He played only six seasons, and at age 27 had barely approached his peak, but Reggie Lewis left his imprint on Celtics history. The quiet Celtic with the infectious smile crammed a lot of memorable basketball into those too-few seasons. It's that and more—all the would-haves and should-haves in a career tragically cut short. Of all the Celtics stars' retired numerals, number 35 stands apart from the others. Seventeen focus on what was, one on what might have been.

Lewis had climbed one plateau after another as he improved consistently and became a Celtics presence. He was the torchbearer to a new Green generation, the leader seemed destined to guide the team back to the top. Hauntingly, Reggie was marking his first playoff game as team captain when he collapsed on the Garden parquet that April night in 1993 during what proved his final game. There is no telling what mountains Lewis would have scaled—on and off the basketball court. "Reggie had it all in front of him," Dave Cowens has said. Lewis already had written one success story—making good with basketball's most glamorous team in his adopted hometown, where he had starred as a collegian. The Northeastern legend not only proved he could play in the NBA but star in a double role.

He was a wiry 6-foot-7 swingman—athletic, aggressive, and effective as the big guard or the small forward. Upfront, his quickness gave him an edge on bigger, slower opponents; in the backcourt, he had an advantage in jumping and size. "Lewis brought one of the quickest first steps seen in

a Celtics uniform in years," Bob Ryan wrote. "He could drive, and he could stop on a dime for crisp 15-foot jumpers. Reggie wasn't afraid to put it up."

As the team's top 1987 draftee, Lewis mostly sat and watched as a rookie. While other NBA rookies must adjust to the pro game at one position, Reggie was preparing for a double role. "We see Reggie as an important part of our future," Jimmy Rodgers said when he took over the coaching reins the next season—an assessment Lewis made good on immediately. Just six games into the schedule, Larry Bird was scratched for the season after surgery. Lewis stepped in and averaged 18.5 points a game. And that was just the start as Reggie blossomed, improving year after year, "just getting better and better," marvelled Red Auerbach, not the only one impressed. "I was a Reggie fan from the day he joined the ball club," Bird wrote in his 1989 autobiography. "With me out, Reggie got a chance to play and proved he was a great scorer . . . he's going to be a great player in this league for many years . . . Reggie's going to be a star."

Lewis soon was, as he became a dominant player and All-Star Game participant, the Celtics' go-to shooter. When a big basket was needed, more often than not his number was called. "You know you're always in a game with Reggie," said backcourt partner Dee Brown, adding the ultimate tribute: "It's like when Larry was playing."

By now, it was 1992–93 and Bird was gone—passing on the captaincy to the soft-spoken Lewis, who relished the role as "another challenge" as he joined a select parade of Celtics drum majors over the years: Cousy, Russell, Havlicek, Cowens, and Bird. He was the shyest of that bunch, which bothered Auerbach not at all. "Reggie doesn't say a lot of words," Red shrugged, "he lets his game speak for him."

And Lewis did while again leading the Celtics in a variety of categories, including a second straight 20-plus scoring season to be among the league's best shooters.

All the while Reggie was proving himself a Hall of Famer in the community.

And suddenly—stunningly—Reggie Lewis was gone.

"What we have left are memories," head scout Rick Weitzman says. "Great memories." ♣

THE
BOSTON
CELTICS
A COMPLETE TEAM PORTFOLIO
Fifty Years

Fifty seasons. Fifty team pictures.

And so much more.

Laid out ahead is the time line of the Boston Celtics, chronicled by the annual team pictures.

Actually, it is more of a bloodline.

The Boston Celtics of 1995-96 were direct decendants of those original Boston Celtics of 1946-47.

Fifty seasons. Sixteen world championships. Twenty-four division titles. A thousand more victories than defeats.

Walter Brown's dream in 1946 became Red Auerbach's quest in 1950.

And the legacy was passed team-by-team, player-by-player—from Russell to Cowens to Parish . . . Ramsey and Heinsohn to Havlicek and Sanders to

Bird and McHale . . . Cousy and Sharman to K.C. and Sam to Jo Jo and DJ . . . to Reggie Lewis and beyond.

All-stars all. Yet none bigger than the team or the tradition.

Certainly no organization in professional sports has enjoyed a greater rate of success over such an extended period of time. But the story of the

Boston Celtics is about so much more—Boston Garden, the parquet, the banners, Red's cigars . . . and all the fans.

Over the 50 seasons, 269 players have worn the green-and-white. Here's a glimpse of each taken as the legacy unfolds . . . one year, one

chapter at a time.

1952-53

L to R (Front Row): Ken Rollins, Bob Donham, Harvey Cohn, Red Auerbach, Bob Cousy, Bill Sharman.
L to R (Back Row): Bob Brannum, Jon Mahnken, Ed Macauley, Walter Brown, Gene Conley, Bob Harris, Chuck Cooper.

1953-54

L to R (Front Row): Bill Sharman, Bob Cousy, Red Auerbach, Bob Donham, Ernie Barrett. L to R (Back Row): Harvey Cohn, Bob Brannum, Bob Harris, Ed Macauley, Jack Nichols, Don Barksdale, Chuck Cooper, Walter Brown.

1954-55

L to R (Front Row): Fred Scolari, Togo Palazzi, Walter Brown, Red Auerbach, Bill Sharman, Bob Cousy.
L to R (Back Row): Harvey Cohn, Frank Ramsey, Dwight Morrison, Ed Macauley, Jack Nichols, Don Barksdale, Bob Brannum.

1955-56

L to R (Front Row): Jim Loscutoff, Jack Nichols, Walter Brown, Red Auerbach, Ed Macauley, Arnie Risen.
L to R (Back Row): Harvey Cohn, Bill Sharman, Ernie Barrett, Dwight Morrison, Dick Hemric, Togo Palazzi, Bob Cousy.

World 1956-57 Champions

L to R (Front Row): Lou Tsioropoulos, Andy Phillip, Frank Ramsey, Red Auerbach, Bob Cousy, Bill Sharman, Jim Loscutoff. L to R (Back Row): Walter Brown, Dick Hemric, Jack Nichols, Bill Russell, Arnie Risen, Tommy Heinsohn, Harvey Cohn, Lou Pieri.

1957-58

L to R (Front Row): Frank Ramsey, Andy Phillip, Walter Brown, Red Auerbach, Lou Pieri, Bob Cousy, Bill Sharman. L to R (Back Row): Lou Tsioropoulos, Jim Loscutoff, Jack Nichols, Bill Russell, Arnie Risen, Tom Heinsohn, Sam Jones, Harvey Cohn.

WORLD 1958-59 CHAMPIONS

L to R (Front Row): (inset) Lou Pieri, Gene Conley, Bob Cousy, Red Auerbach, Walter Brown, Bill Sharman, Bill Russell.
L to R (Back Row): Buddy LeRoux, K. C. Jones, Lou Tsioropoulos, Tom Heinsohn, Ben Swain, Jim Loscutoff, Sam Jones, Frank Ramsey.

WORLD 1959-60 CHAMPIONS

L to R (Front Row): Frank Ramsey, Bob Cousy, Red Auerbach, Walter Brown, Lou Pieri, K. C. Jones, Bill Sharman. L to R (Back Row): Gene Guarilia, Tom Heinsohn, John Richter, Bill Russell, Gene Conley, Jim Loscutoff, Sam Jones, Buddy LeRoux.

WORLD 1960-61 CHAMPIONS

L to R (Front Row): (inset) Lou Pieri, K. C. Jones, Bob Cousy, Red Auerbach, Walter Brown, Bill Sharman, Frank Ramsey.
L to R (Back Row): Buddy LeRoux, Tom Sanders, Tom Heinsohn, Gene Conley, Bill Russell, Gene Guarilia, Jim Loscutoff, Sam Jones.

WORLD 1961-62 CHAMPIONS

L to R (Front Row): K. C. Jones, Gary Phillips, Walter Brown, Red Auerbach, Lou Pieri, Bob Cousy Sam Jones. L to R (Back Row): Frank Ramsey, Tom Sanders, Tom Heinsohn, Bill Russell, Gene Guarilia, Jim Loscutoff, Carl Braun, Buddy LeRoux.

WORLD 1962-63 CHAMPIONS

L to R (Front Row): K. C. Jones, Bill Russell, Walter Brown, Red Auerbach, Lou Pieri, Bob Cousy, Sam Jones. L to R (Back Row): Frank Ramsey, Gene Guarilia, Tom Sanders, Tom Heinsohn, Clyde Lovellette, John Havlicek, Jim Loscutoff, Dan Swartz, Buddy LeRoux.

WORLD 1963-64 CHAMPIONS

L to R (Front Row): Sam Jones, Frank Ramsey, K. C. Jones, Red Auerbach, Walter Brown, Bill Russell, John Havlicek. L to R (Back Row): John McCarthy, Tom Sanders, Tom Heinsohn, Clyde Lovellette, Willie Naulls, Jim Loscutoff, Larry Siegfried, Buddy LeRoux.

WORLD 1964-65 CHAMPIONS

L to R (Front Row): K. C. Jones, Tom Heinsohn, Lou Pieri, Red Auerbach, Bill Russell, Sam Jones. L to R (Back Row): Ron Bonham, Larry Siegfried, Willie Naulls, Mel Counts, John Thompson, Tom Sanders, John Havlicek, Buddy LeRoux.

WORLD 1965-66 CHAMPIONS

L to R (Front Row): John Havlicek, K. C. Jones, Marvin Kratter, Red Auerbach, Jack Waldron, Bill Russell. L to R (Back Row): Ron Bonham, Don Nelson, Tom Sanders, Mel Counts, John Thompson, Woody Sauldsberry, Willie Naulls, Sam Jones, Larry Siegfried, Buddy LeRoux.

1966-67

L to R (Front Row): John Havlicek, K. C. Jones, Jack Waldron, Marvin Kratter, Red Auerbach, Bill Russell, Sam Jones. L to R (Back Row): Bailey Howell, Don Nelson, Tom Sanders, Larry Siegfried, Toby Kimball, Wayne Embry, Ron Watts, Jim Barnett, Joe DeLauri.

WORLD 1967-68 CHAMPIONS

L to R (Front Row): Sam Jones, Larry Siegfried, Red Auerbach, Marvin Kratter, Clarence Adams, Bill Russell, John Havlicek. L to R (Back Row): Joe DeLauri, Rick Weitzman, Tom Thacker, Tom Sanders, Bailey Howell, Wayne Embry, Don Nelson, John Jones, Mel Graham.

WORLD 1968-69 CHAMPIONS

L to R (Front Row): Don Nelson, Sam Jones, Bill Russell, Jack Waldron, Red Auerbach, John Havlicek, Dr. Thomas Silva, Larry Siegfried. L to R (Back Row): Joe DeLauri, Emmette Bryant, Don Chaney, Tom Sanders, Rich Johnson, Jim Barnes, Bailey Howell, Mal Graham.

1969-70

L to R (Front Row): Don Nelson, Woody Erdman, Red Auerbach, John Havlicek, Tom Heinsohn, Jack Waldron, Larry Siegfried. L to R (Back Row): Joe DeLauri, Steve Kuberski, Don Chaney, Jo Jo White, Tom Sanders, Rich Niemann, Rich Johnson, Hank Finkel, Emmett Bryant, Bailey Howell, Jim Barnes, Dr. Thomas Silva.

1946-47

L to R (Front Row): Dutch Garfinkel, Charlie Hoefer, Honey Russell, John Simmons, Wyndol Gray.
L to R (Back Row): Harvey Cohn, Al Brightman, Art Spector, Harold Kottman, Connie Simmons, Gerard Kelly, Danny Silva.

1947-48

L to R (Front Row): Saul Mariaschin, George Munroe, Cecil Hankins, Honey Russell. Dutch Garfinkel, Mel Riebe, Chuck Hoefer.
L to R (Back Row): Harvey Cohn, Gene Stump, Eddie Ehlers, Art Spector, Connie Simmons, Ed Sadowski, Chuck Connors, John Janisch.

1948-49

L to R (Front Row): Art Spector, Eddie Ehlers, George Kaftan, Doggie Julian, Dermie O'Connell, Gene Stump, Jim Seminoff.
L to R (Back Row): Phil Farbman, Bob Doll, George Nostrand, Bob Kinney, John Ezersky.

1949-50

L to R (Top Row): Walter Brown, Dermie O'Connell, John Mahnken, Doggie Julian. L to R (Middle Row): Brady Walker, Joe Mullaney, Bob Doll, Tony Lavelli, Ed Leede. L to R (Bottom Row): George Kaftan, Howie Shannon, Bob Kinney, Sonny Hertzberg, Jim Seminoff.

1950-51

L to R (Front Row): Ed Stanczak, Bob Cousy, Walter Brown, Sonny Hertzberg, Red Auerbach, Bob Donham, Ed Leede.
L to R (Back Row): Harvey Cohn, Bob Harris, Ed Macauley, John Mahnken, Harry Boykoff, Chuck Cooper.

1951-52

L to R (Front Row): EdMacauley, Lou Pieri, Red Auerbach, Walter Brown, "Bones" McKinney.
L to R (Back Row): Dick Dickey, Bill Sharman, Bob Donham, Chuck Cooper, John Mahnken, Bob Harris, Bob Brannum, Bob Cousy, Harvey Cohn.

1988-89

L to R (Front Row): Kelvin Upshaw, Brian Shaw, Kevin McHale, Alan Cohen, Jan Volk, Red Auerbach, Jim Rodgers, Don Gaston, Robert Parish, Larry Bird, Dennis Johnson. L to R (Back Row): Wayne Lebeaux, Dr. Arnold Scheller, Lanny Van Eman, Otis Birdsong, Reggie Lewis, Ron Grandison, Ramon Rivas, Mark Acres, Joe Kleine, Ed Pinckney, Jim Paxson, Kevin Gamble, Chris Ford, Ed Lacerte.

1989-90

L to R (Front Row): Kelvin Upshaw, Dennis Johnson, Kevin McHale, Alan Cohen, Jan Volk, Red Auerbach, Jim Rodgers, Don Gaston, Robert Parish, Larry Bird, Charles Smith. L to R (Back Row): Wayne Lebeaux, John Bagley, Dr. Arnold Scheller, Lanny Van Eman, Kevin Gamble, Reggie Lewis, Michael Smith, Joe Kleine, Ed Pinckney, Jim Paxson, Chris Ford, Ed Lacerte.

1990-91

L to R (Front Row): John Bagley, Reggie Lewis, Kevin McHale, Alan Cohen, Jan Volk, Red Auerbach, Dave Gavitt, Chris Ford, Don Gaston, Larry Bird, Robert Parish, Dee Brown. L to R (Back Row): Wayne Lebeaux, Dr. Arnold Scheller, Jon Jennings, Kevin Gamble, Ed Pinckney, Dave Popson, Stojko Vrankovic, Joe Kleine, Michael Smith, Brian Shaw, Charles Smith, Don Casey, Ed Lacerte.

1991-92

L to R (Front Row): John Bagley, Kevin McHale, Alan Cohen, Jan Volk, Dave Gavitt, Red Auerbach, Chris Ford, Don Gaston, Larry Bird, Robert Parish. L to R (Back Row): Wayne Lebeaux, Jon Jennings, Dee Brown, Kevin Gamble, Reggie Lewis, Joe Kleine, Stojko Vrankovic, Ed Pinckney, Rick Fox, Sherman Douglas, Don Casey, Dr. Arnold Scheller, Ed Lacerte.

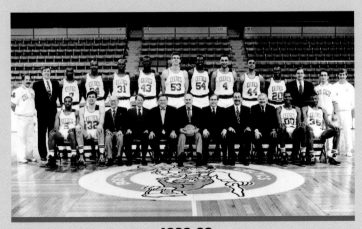

1992-93

L to R (Front Row): John Bagley, Kevin McHale, Alan Cohen, Paul Dupee, Dave Gavitt, Red Auerbach, Jan Volk, Chris Ford, Don Gaston, Robert Parish, Reggie Lewis. L to R (Back Row): Wayne Lebeaux, Don Casey, Dee Brown, Kevin Gamble, Xavier McDaniel, Lorenzo Williams, Joe Kleine, Ed Pinckney, Alaa Abdelnaby, Rick Fox, Sherman Douglas, Jon Jennings, Ed Lacerte, Vladimir Shulman.

1993-94

L to R (Front Row): Dee Brown, Robert Parish, Paul Gaston, Dave Gavitt, Red Auerbach, Jan Volk, Chris Ford, Steve Schram, Sherman Douglas, Kevin Gamble. L to R (Back Row): Dr. Arnold Scheller, Jon Jennings, Dennis Johnson, Jimmy Oliver, Rick Fox, Ed Pinckney, Dino Radja, Acie Earl, Matt Wenstrom, Alaa Abdelnaby, Xavier McDaniel, Chris Corchiani, Don Casey, Ed Lacerte, Wayne Lebeaux.

1970-71

L to R (Front Row): Don Nelson, Woody Erdman, Red Auerbach, John Havlicek, Tom Heinsohn, Dr. Thomas Silva, Tom Sanders.
L to R (Back Row): Joe DeLauri, Art Williams, Bill Dinwiddie, Steve Kuberski, Garfield Smith, Hank Finkel, Dave Cowens, Willie Williams, Don Chaney, Rex Morgan, Jo Jo White.

1971-72

L to R (Front Row): Jo Jo White, Tom Heinsohn, John Havlicek, Red Auerbach, Tom Sanders, Dr. Thomas Silva, Don Nelson.
L to R (Back Row): Mark Volk, Art Williams, Rex Morgan, Clarence Glover, Steve Kuberski, Hank Finkel, Dave Cowens, Garfield Smith, Don Chaney, Frank Challant.

1972-73

L to R (Front Row): Don Chaney, Don Nelson, Robert Schmertz, Red Auerbach, John Havlicek, Tom Heinsohn, John Killilea, Tom Sanders, Jo Jo White. L to R (Back Row): Mark Volk, Dr. Sam Kane, Art Williams, Paul Westphal, Mark Minor, Paul Silas, Hank Finkel, Dave Cowens, Steve Kuberski, Dr. Thomas Silva, Frank Challant.

WORLD 1973-74 CHAMPIONS

L to R (Front Row): Jo Jo White, Don Chaney, John Havlicek, Red Auerbach, Bob Schmertz, Tom Heinsohn, Dave Cowens, Paul Silas, John Killilea. L to R (Back Row): Mark Volk, Dr. Sam Kane, Paul Westphal, Phil Hankinson, Steve Downing, Don Nelson, Hank Finkel, Steve Kuberski, Art Williams, Dr. Thomas Silva, Frank Challant.

1974-75

L to R (Front Row): Jo Jo White, John Havlicek, Red Auerbach, Bob Schmertz, Tom Heinsohn, Paul Silas, Don Chaney, Dave Cowens.
L to R (Back Row): Dr. Sam Kane, Mark Volk, Kevin Stacom, Glenn McDonald, Paul Westphal, Jim Ard, Hank Finkel, Don Nelson, Ben Clyde, Phil Hankinson, Frank Challant, Dr. Thomas Silva.

WORLD 1975-76 CHAMPIONS

L to R (Front Row): Charlie Scott, Paul Silas, Dave Cowens, Irving Levin, Tom Heinsohn, Arnold Red Auerbach, John Havlicek, Jo Jo White, Don Nelson. L to R (Back Row): Dr. Thomas Silva, Mark Volk, Kevin Stacom, Glenn McDonald, Tom Boswell, Jim Ard, Steve Kuberski, Jerome Anderson, Frank Challant, Dr. Sam Kane.

1976-77

L to R (Front Row): Dave Cowens, Jo Jo White, Red Auerbach, Tom Heinsohn, Irving Levin, John Havlicek, Jim Ard. L to R (Back Row): Mark Volk, Dr. Thomas Silva, Kevin Stacom, Norm Cook, Sidney Wicks, Tom Boswell, Steve Kuberski, Curtis Rowe, Fred Saunders, John Killilea, Frank Challant, Dr. Sam Kane, Inset-Charlie Scott.

1977-78

L to R (Front Row): Dave Cowens, Red Auerbach, John Havlicek, Irving Levin, Tom Sanders, Jo Jo White. L to R (Back Row): Dr. Thomas Silva, Ernie DiGregorio, Kevin Stacom, Dave Bing, Don Chaney, Curtis Rowe, Sidney Wicks, Tom Boswell, Kermit Washington, Cedric Maxwell, Frank Challant, Dr. Sam Kane.

1978-79

L to R (Front Row): Chris Ford, Red Auerbach, Dave Cowens, Harry Mangurian Jr., Don Chaney. L to R (Back Row): K. C. Jones, Kevin Stacom, Frankie Sanders, Jeff Judkins, Curtis Rowe, Rick Robey, Bob McAdoo, Cedric Maxwell, Nate Archibald, Frank Challant, Bob MacKinnon.

1979-80

L to R (Front Row): Cedric Maxwell, K. C. Jones, Harry Mangurian Jr., Dave Cowens, Red Auerbach, Bill Fitch, Don Chaney. L to R (Back Row): Gerald Henderson, M. L. Carr, Larry Bird, Rick Robey, Eric Fernsten, Jeff Judkins, Chris Ford, Nate Archibald, Ray Melchiorre.

World 1980-81 Champions

L to R (Front Row): Chris Ford, Cedric Maxwell, Red Auerbach, Bill Fitch, Harry Mangurian Jr., Larry Bird, Nate Archibald. L to R (Back Row): K. C. Jones, Wayne Kreklow, M. L. Carr, Rick Robey, Robert Parish, Kevin McHale, Eric Fernsten, Gerald Henderson, Jim Rodgers, Ray Melchiorre.

1981-82

L to R (Front Row): Cedric Maxwell, Chris Ford, M. L. Carr, Red Auerbach, Bill Fitch, Harry Mangurian Jr., Nate Archibald, Larry Bird, Gerald Henderson. L to R (Back Row): K. C. Jones, Terry Duerod, Danny Ainge, Kevin McHale, Robert Parish, Rick Robey, Eric Fernsten, Charles Bradley, Ray Melchiorre, Jim Rodgers.

1982-83

L to R (Front Row): Quinn Buckner, M. L. Carr, Larry Bird, Red Auerbach, Harry Mangurian Jr., Bill Fitch, Cedric Maxwell, Nate Archibald, Gerald Henderson. L to R (Back Row): Dr. Thomas Silva, K. C. Jones, Danny Ainge, Kevin McHale, Robert Parish, Rick Robey, Scott Wedman, Charles Bradley, Jim Rodgers, Ray Melchiorre.

World 1983-84 Champions

L to R (Front Row): Quinn Buckner, Cedric Maxwell, Paul R. Dupee, Don Gaston, Red Auerbach, K. C. Jones, Alan Cohen, Larry Bird, M. L. Carr. L to R (Back Row): Dr. Thomas Silva, Jim Rodgers, Gerald Henderson, Scott Wedman, Greg Kite, Robert Parish, Kevin McHale, Dennis Johnson, Danny Ainge, Carlos Clark, Chris Ford, Ray Melchiorre.

1984-85

L to R(Front Row): Quinn Buckner, Cedric Maxwell, Alan Cohen, Jan Volk, Red Auerbach, K. C. Jones, Don Gaston, Paul R. Dupee, Larry Bird, M. L. Carr. L to R (Back Row): Ed Badger, Jim Rodgers, Ray Williams, Danny Ainge, Scott Wedman, Greg Kite, Robert Parish, Kevin McHale, Rick Carlisle, Dennis Johnson, Carlos Clark, Chris Ford, Ray Melchiorre.

World 1985-86 Champions

L to R (Front Row): Danny Ainge, Scott Wedman, Alan Cohen, Jan Volk, Red Auerbach, K. C. Jones, Don Gaston, Larry Bird, Dennis Johnson. L to R (Back Row): Wayne Lebeaux, Dr. Thomas Silva, Jim Rodgers, Sam Vincent, Rick Carlisle, Greg Kite, Robert Parish, Bill Walton, Kevin McHale, David Thirdkill, Jerry Sichting, Chris Ford, Ray Melchiorre.

1986-87

L to R (Front Row): Sam Vincent, Danny Ainge, Scott Wedman, Alan Cohen, Jan Volk, Red Auerbach, K. C. Jones, Don Gaston, Larry Bird, Dennis Johnson, Jerry Sichting. L to R (Back Row): Wayne Lebeaux, Dr. Thomas Silva, Jim Rodgers, Conner Henry, Greg Kite, Kevin McHale, Robert Parish, Bill Walton, Fred Roberts, Darren Daye, Rick Carlisle, Chris Ford, Ray Melchiorre.

1987-88

L to R (Front Row): Dirk Minniefield, Danny Ainge, Kevin McHale, Alan Cohen, Jan Volk, Red Auerbach, K. C. Jones, Don Gaston, Robert Parish, Larry Bird, Dennis Johnson. L to R (Back Row): Wayne Lebeaux, Dr. Arnold Scheller, Jim Rodgers, Jim Paxson, Mark Acres, Bill Walton, Artis Gilmore, Brad Lohaus, Fred Roberts, Reggie Lewis, Chris Ford, Ed Lacerte.

1994-95

1995-96

L to R (Front Row): Dee Brown, Dominique Wilkins, Jan Volk, M. L. Carr, Red Auerbach, Paul Gaston, Chris Ford, Paul Dupee Jr., Steve Schram, Xavier McDaniel, Sherman Douglas. L to R (Back Row): Ed Lacerte, Dr. Arnold Scheller, Dennis Johnson, David Wesley, Greg Minor, Rick Fox, Dino Radja, Pervis Ellison, Eric Montross, Acie Earl, Derek Strong, Jay Humphries, Don Casey, Wayne Lebeaux, Vladimir Shulman.

L to R (Front Row): David Wesley, Greg Minor, Rick Fox, Jan Volk, M.L. Carr, Red Auerbach, Paul Gaston, Steve Schram, Dee Brown, Todd Day, Dana Barros. L to R (Back Row): Dr. Arnold Scheller, Ed Lacerte, Dennis Johnson, Eric Williams, Pervis Ellision, Alton Lister, Thomas Hamilton, Eric Montross, Dino Radja, Todd Mundt, Doug Smith, Junior Burrough, John Kuester, Don Casey, Wayne Lebeaux, Validimir Schulman.

Their numbers are retired …

> *Their accomplishments are not forgotten.*

| 1945 | 1950 | 1955 | 1960 | 1965 | 1970 | 1975 | 1980 | 1985 | 1990 | 1995 | 2000 |

1 Walter Brown, owner / president, 1946-1964 (7 championships)

2 Red Auerbach, coach / general manager / president, 1950- (16 championships)

14 Bob Cousy, player, 1950-51–1962-63 (6 championships)

22 Ed Macauley, player, 1950-51–1955-56

21 Bill Sharman, player, 1951-52–1960-61 (4 championships)

23 Frank Ramsey, player, 1954-55–1963-64 (7 championships)

Loscy Jim Loscutoff, player, 1955-56–1963-64 (7 championships)

6 Bill Russell, player / coach, 1956-57–1968-69 (11 championships)

15 Tom Heinsohn, player / coach, 1956-57–1964-65, 1969-70–1977-78 (10 championships)

24 Sam Jones, player, 1957-58—1968-69 (10 championships)

25 K. C. Jones, player / coach, 1958-59—1966-67, 1983-84–1987-88 (11 championships)*

16 Tom "Satch" Sanders, player / coach, 1960-61–1972-73, 1977-78–1978-79 (8 championships)

17 John Havlicek, player, 1962-63–1977-78 (8 championships)

19 Don Nelson, player, 1965-66–1975-76 (5 championships)

10 Jo Jo White, player, 1969-70–1978-79 (2 championships)

18 Dave Cowens, player-coach, 1970-71–1979-80 (2 championships)

33 Larry Bird, player, 1979-80–1991-92 (3 championships)

32 Kevin McHale, player, 1980-81–1992-93 (3 championships)

3 Dennis Johnson, player, 1983-84–1989-90 (2 championships)

35 Reggie Lewis, player, 1987-88–1992-93

* Jones' 11 championships includes the 1981 season as an assistant coach.

TOP TEN MATCHUPS AND RIVALRIES

BY BOB RYAN

A basic element of professional basketball is the man-to-man matchup, a crucial ingredient of the bigger picture—the pairing of teams. Here's a veteran observer's view of the ten greatest matchups and team rivalries in Celtics history.

GREAT MATCHUPS

BOB COUSY
VS.
SLATER MARTIN
1950–60

Slater "Dugie" Martin never averaged more than 13 points per game, but points were not what this dynamic Texan was all about.

Martin was a feisty 5-foot-9 guard who personified the term "sparkplug." He was always among the league's leaders in assists and played tough, hard-nosed, belly-to-belly defense, and this is the quality which made him such a memorable opponent for Cousy. The rivalry began when Cousy entered the NBA in 1950, and in the beginning the team satisfaction all belonged to Martin, whose Minneapolis Lakers won the title in 1950, 1952, 1953, and 1954.

The rivalry continued anew when Martin was traded to the St. Louis Hawks in December 1956. He assumed leadership of that team, playing in the finals against the Celtics in 1957, 1958, and 1960, and earning a fifth championship ring in 1958.

Slater Martin made Bob Cousy work harder than any man he ever faced.

BILL RUSSELL
VS.
WILT CHAMBERLAIN
1959–69

An unarguable premise: this was the greatest individual matchup in NBA history.

No confrontation has ever sparked more barroom arguments. Would Russell have propelled Philadelphia/San Francisco/Los Angeles to anywhere near as many titles (11) as the Celtics won with him? Would Red Auerbach and Wilt have gotten along? Did Russell really stop Wilt, or did the Celtics simply play better team defense? Does Wilt's overwhelming statistical superiority in their head-to-head battles mean what Wilt says it means, or does Russell's far better win-loss record in those little wars say it all?

It was a glamorized match-up from the get-go, and not just because the two were clearly the two best centers alive in the fifties and sixties. The fact that Boston and Philadelphia were such blood rivals made it more interesting than it would have been if the two played for, say, Rochester and Syracuse. When it ended, Wilt was in Los Angeles.

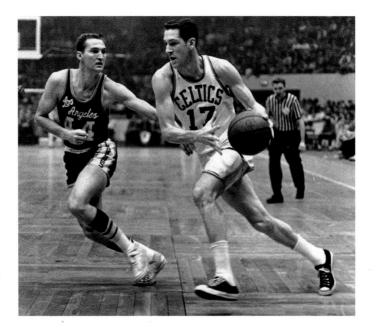

JOHN HAVLICEK
VS.
JERRY WEST
1962–74

West was already established as one of the two best guards in basketball (along with Oscar Robertson) when Havlicek came out of Ohio State to join the Celtics as a frisky pup without a true position. No one foresaw the path this superb rivalry would take.

Havlicek came into the pros as a running forward without much of a jump shot, but he worked to develop his perimeter skills, and in so doing inevitably found himself matched up with West for major portions of ballgames. There was no better treat for the basketball aficionado of the sixties, for the 6-foot-3 West and the 6-foot-5 Havlicek were the two best all-around players of their day.

West was fated to play the Don Quixote role, tilting against the Celtics windmill of the sixties. He went into the finals six times against the Celtics without ever experiencing team success. But his virtuosity earned him enormous respect.

A typical West-Havlicek confrontation was Game 1 of the 1969 finals. West had 53; Havlicek had 41. The Lakers prevailed in that game, but Boston won the series in seven.

JOHN HAVLICEK
VS.
BILL BRADLEY
1967–76

Hondo never had either a more tenacious or a smarter foe at small forward than the future senator from New Jersey.

Bradley was unique in that he mirrored Havlicek in his uncanny ability to get himself open. No two players in the game moved better without the ball than John Havlicek and Bill Bradley, so when the Celtics and the Knicks played in those days the subplot small forward was juicy indeed.

Bradley wasn't all that quick, so he needed to employ every defensive tactic imaginable. Hence the following practice exchange between Celtics coach Tom Heinsohn and Havlicek:

Heinsohn: "John, I can't stand the way that Bradley guards you. The next time he puts two hands on your hips, I want you to take the basketball and smash it in his face!"

Havlicek: "But, Tommy, it doesn't bother me at all."

DAVE COWENS
VS.
KAREEM ABDUL-JABBAR
1970–80

This (literal) David and Goliath confrontation helped define Cowens as the

NBA's fiercest competitor.

The 6-foot-8 Cowens accepted the challenge of trying to contain the 7-foot-3 Kareem without complaint. In fact, he thrived on it. The Cowens rationale was that if he couldn't be as tall as Kareem, or as reliable with the hook shot, he'd gain parity by being a better rebounder, a better outside shooter, a better runner up and down the floor, and, in general terms, a just plain tougher guy.

Many a Celtics-Bucks (and, later, Lakers) game in the seventies came down to this: It's the fourth quarter and Cowens is still running up and down the floor and Kareem isn't. Sure, some came down to the idea that it's the fourth quarter and Kareem is sinking his hook shot and there is nothing Cowens can do about it. Just let the record show that by 1976, after Kareem had been in the league for seven years and Cowens had been in the league for six, Cowens had two titles to his credit and Kareem had one. Cowens always made Kareem work harder than he really wanted to, and Cowens knew it.

DAVE COWENS
VS.
BOB MCADOO
1972–80

Central casting could not possibly have sent over a more polar opposite puzzle—call it the anti-Kareem—for Cowens to solve than Bob McAdoo.

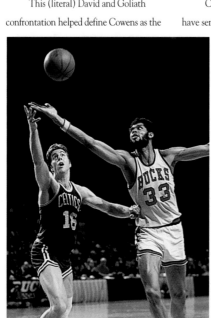

In the McAdoo confrontation, Cowens was the bruiser. In the McAdoo confrontation, the Buffalo center was the better outside shooter. Cowens was the hunter and McAdoo was the rabbit.

The 6-foot-9 McAdoo broke into the NBA as a forward in 1972. But when the Braves traded 7-foot Elmore Smith to Los Angeles, the slender sharpshooter became a center, and thus became Cowens' responsibility. In their first regular season meeting of the

'73–74 season, McAdoo dropped 49 on Cowens' head, and the rivalry was on.

There were memorable playoff meetings in '74 and '76. Cowens took over one game with a 20-point, nine-rebound, three-block fourth quarter, but McAdoo always kept firing away. You'd think Cowens could block McAdoo's shot every once in a while, but no matter how high Cowens jumped, McAdoo always got off his shot.

The flip side was that McAdoo couldn't stop the Cowens jump hook.

LARRY BIRD
VS.
MICHAEL COOPER
1979–90

Number 33 saw a lot of them come and go, but there wasn't anyone he was happier to see head for the Happy Hunting Ground of Hoopdom than the skinny piece of human velcro who went by the name of Michael Cooper.

It wasn't a strict two-way matchup, but few of Bird's were, really. The nature of the Celtics frontcourt dictated many crossover matchups, so both Bird and Kevin McHale guarded men who didn't guard them back. But one thing was certain during the eighties; namely, that Michael Cooper would be the man guarding Larry Bird, especially when the Lakers were in trouble.

At 6-foot-5, Cooper's calling cards were great quickness and great intelligence. He would work tirelessly to deny Bird the basketball, and he accomplished his task better than anyone. On offense he also made the Celtics squirm with his deadly three-point shooting.

When people would credit others with the ability to stop Bird, Larry would always bristle. "Michael Cooper is the best defender alive," he would say, and that would end the discussion.

KEVIN MCHALE
VS.
CHARLES BARKLEY
1984–93

It was the late winter of 1984. They

were sitting around the hotel in Milwaukee when then, assistant coach Chris Ford walked into the lobby. "Where've you been?" inquired Kevin McHale.

"I've just been to the SEC tourney," Ford replied, "and I saw the guy who's going to kick your butt for the next 10 years."

He was talking about a kid from Auburn named Charles Barkley, who then weighed about 300 pounds and was known as the "Round Mountain of Rebound."

Barkley may not have kicked Kevin's butt for the next 10 years, but not because he didn't try. Amid the gigantic assortment of body sizes and temperaments McHale would find himself confronted with during his career, there was no more interesting challenge to him than the one offered by the 6-foot-5 Barkley, whose combination of inside moves, drives, and bombs from beyond the arc, made Barkley a fascinating matchup.

For his part, Barkley frequently cited McHale as his single toughest opponent.

ROBERT PARISH
VS.
BILL LAIMBEER

It was always the great nonmoment of the eighties and early nineties. Parish and Laimbeer stand at midcourt prior to the opening tap of an eagerly awaited clash. Laimbeer sticks out his hand. Parish gazes toward the ceiling. Robert Parish would sooner have poured salsa on his new three-piece suit than have shaken hands with Bill Laimbeer.

Parish believed Laimbeer was a dirty player. Laimbeer didn't care what Parish, or anyone else, thought. He just set about the business of being Bill Laimbeer, which meant rebounding hard at both ends, setting rugged picks, and making irritating tippy-toe jumpers from mid- or long-range. Parish would likewise be Parish, which meant posting up for those rainbow turnarounds, throwing in those hooks or jump-hooks, and, of course, running the floor for sneakaway layups.

The feud—OK, one-way feud—

reached a new level in 1987 when Parish, infuriated by what he believed were improper Laimbeer elbows, simply began whaling away at his hated rival with the old one-two. Amazingly, the referees never saw

it. In the aftermath of it all, however, Parish was suspended for a game. This elicited one of the great lines in the history of the franchise. Apprised that Parish had been suspended for punching Laimbeer, general

manager Jan Volk observed, "Parish is suspended, but the consummate provocateur is still roaming the hardwoods."

Ah, those were the days.

DENNIS JOHNSON
vs.
MAGIC JOHNSON
1983–90

When people see the name Magic Johnson, they could normally expect to see it followed by the name Larry Bird. But theirs was a parallel rivalry, not a direct matchup. It was something for the headline writers to savor.

The true matchup of the day took place in the backcourt: Johnson vs. Johnson. When the Celtics acquired Dennis Johnson from Phoenix in that

lopsided trade for Rick Robey, they got more than a high-profile scorer and passer. They got a guy who wasn't afraid of Magic Johnson.

DJ didn't always guard Magic in the beginning, because K. C. Jones was a peculiar coach. But DJ guarded Magic when things got sticky, and he was on him like a lead overcoat in Games 4 through 7 of the 1984 Finals. It may have been his finest hour as a Celtic, as he kept Magic in check at the defensive end while scoring 20 or more in each game himself.

DJ gave up inches to Magic—who didn't?—but he made up for it with strength, tenacity, and brains. After that, K. C. Jones allowed DJ to guard Magic, and both the fans and the team were better off for it.

GREAT TEAM RIVALRIES

SYRACUSE NATIONALS

Playing in Syracuse was tough.

"You might win in New York occasionally," recalls Bob Cousy. "New York was still the mecca in the early fifties, and we all wanted to show off. But Syracuse was a different matter. There'd be 4,000 people, all shouting obscenities and throwing things. You'd say, 'Why am I here?' The playoffs were different, but you couldn't generate the intensity you needed to win in Syracuse."

Good players had something to do with the Celtics' frustration. The Nats won playoff series over the Celtics in '53, '54, '55, and '56 with players such as Dolph Schayes, Paul Seymour, George King, Red Rocha, and Billy Gabor in the early days. Then came Bill Russell, which was enough to scare most teams. "When Russ came," says The Cooz, "that was the end of New York, and some others. But not Syracuse. They were still good." The rivalry reached an apex in '59 when a Syracuse unit of Schayes, Kerr, George Yardley, Larry Costello, and Hal Greer

took the Celtics to the bridge before losing an epic back-and-forth seventh game (130-125) which remains one of the great playoff games of all time.

ST. LOUIS HAWKS

This flame burned brightly for five seasons as the Hawks and Celtics met for the NBA title four times from 1957-'61.

St. Louis entered the '57 playoffs as a seemingly unworthy 34-48 team, but it eventually took the Celtics seven games and two harrowing overtimes in order to subdue the bucking bronco presented by Bob Pettit, Cliff Hagan, Ed Macauley, Charlie Share, Jack McMahon, Slater Martin, Jack Coleman, and player-coach Alex Hannum. The Hawks showed just how tough they were the following year when Pettit's 50-point performance in Game 6 brought them a championship.

The Hawks were bedeviled by Bill Russell, as was to be expected, but the Celtics had their own problems with the wonderful St. Louis forward tandem of Pettit and Hagan, a pair of physically and mentally tough hombres who feared no man. Martin always held his own against

Bob Cousy, another rarity of the times. After winning the title in '58, St. Louis took the Celtics to a seventh game in '60 and to five in '61. Suffice it to say that this bunch was never in awe of the mighty Boston Celtics.

PHILLY/SAN FRANCISCO WARRIORS
PHILLY 76ERS

Long before I-95 came into existence, there was a strong psychic connection between Philadelphia and Boston. It began to take shape the minute Wilt Chamberlain joined the Warriors in 1959, and it continues to this day.

With Chamberlain came a ready-made rivalry. His battles with Bill Russell are legendary, but there was more to this confrontation. Tom Meschery and Paul Arizin were handfuls for the Celtics forwards. Guy Rodgers matched up very well with Bob Cousy. When Al Attles arrived in 1960, the Warriors now had a serious macho man guard who could take on the Bill Sharmans and Sam Joneses of the world in perpetuity.

The rivalry was smoking from the start, with the teams engaging in a tong war

of six games in 1960, culminating in a two-point Boston victory in the deciding contest. They had an even better seven-gamer two years later, with a Sam Jones banker winning Game 7 by two points.

When the Warriors went west, the rivalry continued, and there was another championship clash in '64. Wilt was traded back to Philly in '65, and that series ended with the famous "Havlicek stole the ball." The 76ers had their greatest moment of elation when they eliminated the Celtics in '67 en route to a title.

In all, these teams met in the playoffs eight times in the sixties, seven in Philly and once in San Francisco. The word "intense" applies.

LOS ANGELES LAKERS
PART I

How could you not feel sorry for the Lakers, as well as for Elgin Baylor and Jerry West? Six times they played the Celtics in the NBA Finals during the sixties, and six times they went home weeping.

No matter what the Lakers did, it wasn't enough. Baylor scoring 61 in a '62 playoff game . . . Frank Selvy's open jumper which could have won the title in '62 . . . A limping and soon-to-be-retiring Bob Cousy leading the Celtics to victory in 1963 . . . West scoring 40 points a game in a five-game defeat in '65 . . . Lakers falling two points short in Game 7 (Red Auerbach's last game) in '66 . . . Havlicek scoring 40 on them in a crucial game in '68 . . . ancient Celtics spotting the Lakers a 2-0 edge and clawing back to win Game 7 in the balloon-laden Forum in '69.

Baylor and West were invariably magnificent, but The Difference was always Bill Russell. L. A. never had a center who could remotely challenge him, and that was that. But no Celtics foes have ever succumbed with more valor than Elgin Baylor and Jerry West.

NEW YORK KNICKS

From 1956 through 1967 the Knicks were no factor—none. The Celtics laughed at them.

But New York got its act together by 1968, and a wonderful rivalry was born. The two met in 1969, with the wily Celtics squirming through in a tough six games. It was clear New York's time had come, and by the following season the world was theirs. Russell and Sam Jones were gone, and now it was New York's turn. Willis Reed, Dave DeBusschere, Bill Bradley, Walt Frazier and Company were in charge.

The great games took place in Boston over the next five years. The Boston Garden was infused with a special energy for Knicks' games, because the New York–bred college kids came out by the thousands to cheer for the Knicks. This lent a college-type atmosphere to the games.

The Knicks prevailed in 1972 and 1973, the latter an especially wrenching loss for the Celtics, who had won 68 regular-season games. Boston reversed the result a year later, when DeBusschere and Reed were injured, as Havlicek had been the year before.

This was as good as any rivalry the Celtics ever had, with superb individual matchups across the board (Cowens-Reed, Silas-DeBusschere, Havlicek-Bradley, Chaney-Frazier, White-Barnett/Monroe).

BUFFALO BRAVES

The Buffalo Braves came into existence in the 1970–71 season and immediately became raw meat for the Celtics, who beat them 22 straight times. But on March 1, 1974, the Braves whacked the Celtics by 16 in Buffalo and an instant rivalry was born.

A brilliant trade which gave the Braves veteran forward Jack Marin made the Braves competitive. They already had Bob McAdoo and Rookie of the Year-to-be Ernie DiGregorio, in addition to guard Randy Smith. The teams hooked up in a torrid playoff series that year, with the Celtics pulling it out in a memorable sixth game, actually decided by two controversial Jo Jo White free throws after the final buzzer. The Braves insisted that the foul called on McAdoo was bogus.

The Cowens/McAdoo and Ernie D-Smith/Havlicek-White-Chaney matchups were spectacular, and for the next two seasons this was a primo rivalry. Each game in both arenas was a sellout, and one night in Buffalo a swaggering Paul Silas inquired how many people were in attendance. About 18,000, he was told.

"Good," he said. "We're going to send them all home unhappy."

There was another tough six-game playoff struggle in '76, but the Buffalo team was broken up the following year, and this short-lived, but sizzling, rivalry was history.

PHILADELPHIA 76ERS
PART II

When Larry Bird joined the Celtics in 1979, the 76ers were up and the Celtics were down. Not for long. For the next half-dozen years both teams were up, and this was an NBA rivalry beyond compare.

The teams were playoff foes in 1980, 1981, 1982, and 1985, each winning two series. The matchups began with Bird and Cedric Maxwell vs. Julius Erving, and they included Darryl Dawkins/Caldwell Jones vs. Kevin McHale/Robert Parish, Moses Malone vs. Parish/McHale, Tiny Archibald vs. Maurice Cheeks, and Andrew (the Boston Strangler) Toney vs. Everyone.

Highlights? Oh, baby. How about the Celtics coming from 3-1 down to win Games 4, 5, and 6 in '81 by margins of 2, 2, and 1? How about Philly winning a Game 7 in Boston a year later when no one on earth except the 12 players and coach Billy Cunningham thought they could? How about the shocking Bird-Erving fight in '85? How about the exhibition game brawl featuring Moses Malone and Red Auerbach himself in '83?

They simply do not get any better than this pairing.

LOS ANGELES LAKERS
PART II

Of course, this hinged on the extraordinary skills and personalities of Bird and Magic, but it was a whole lot more.

The Celtics and Lakers represented totally different cultures and organizational philosophies. It was L. A. glitz and glamour ("Showtime") against traditional eastern propriety—or so it was portrayed. The teams met for the championship in the ballyhooed '84 finals, which the Celtics won in workmanlike fashion despite being outplayed in an aesthetic sense. Pat Riley vowed never again to be out-muscled by anyone, and he wasn't.

Always towering over the proceedings (literally) was Kareem Abdul-Jabbar, who declared his team's 1985 triumph in Boston to be his greatest source of career satisfaction. But the matchups were superb throughout. Bird always acknowledged Michael Cooper as his toughest defensive challenge. James Worthy and Kevin McHale were tremendous forces. Dennis Johnson dueled admirably with Magic.

The "Best of" from this rivalry would be a wonderful video to own.

DETROIT PISTONS

It was a little difficult for Boston fans to take the Pistons seriously as a rival, but it became a whole lot easier when Dennis Rodman showed up.

The Celtics had subdued an offensive-minded Detroit team in six games in '85, but the rivalry took on a new flavor in the '86–87 season when the weird rookie from Southeast Oklahoma showed up to join such ready-made Celtics villains as Bill Laimbeer and Isiah Thomas. The '87 seven-gamer was a phenomenal show which included Parish punching out Laimbeer in Game 5, the famous Bird steal of the Thomas inbound and subsequent feed to a cutting Dennis Johnson for the game-winning basket in the same game, and the glorious seventh game, when Bird led the Celtics to victory and then Rodman and Thomas put him down afterward.

The teams really came to dislike each other intensely, and though the edge had then swung to Detroit, each game was a ferocious struggle, right through the '90–91 season, when the Celtics believed that a bad call by referee Jack Madden wiped out a crucial McHale put-back hoop in overtime of the deciding Game 6, which was eventually won by Detroit.

MILWAUKEE BUCKS

The 1974 finals between the Celtics and Bucks remain a sentimental favorite for all who saw them, but there was more to this on-going rivalry than those seven games.

It was a strange series in which the visiting team won five times. Kareem Abdul-Jabbar was transcendent, averaging 32 points and 12 rebounds a game.

Even with Kareem off to L. A. , Milwaukee remained a threat in the seventies and eighties, and the Celtics had to deal with them in 1983, 1984, 1986, and 1987. The Bucks became the first team ever to sweep the Celtics in four with a stunning triumph in '83, and so it was with immense satisfaction that Boston came back with a 4-1 victory the following year and a convincing sweep of their own a year later (one of Bird's great virtuoso performances). The series was a surprisingly taut seven-gamer, highlighted by an epic 138-137 double-OT victory in Game 4.

The noble Milwaukee figure in the eighties was Sidney Moncrief, a 6-foot-4 guard with a gigantic heart. Parochial Bostonians would say he was a born Celtic.

The Green and White

"As far as basketball is concerned, the greatest thing you can say is that you played for the Boston Celtics."

"Easy Ed" Macauley

THE
CELTICS
LEGACY

"Other teams have history, the Celtics have a mystique."

BOB RYAN

It was an ominous beginning.

There were the 4,329 first-nighters—who paid $1.25, $2 and $2.75 to sit in on history—setting into their seats at Boston Arena minutes before the opening tapoff of professional basketball in Boston on November 5, 1946. And there was Kevin "Chuck" Connors taking a final warmup toss, arching a long two-handed setshot that shattered a glass backboard.

So the Celtics were a *smash* in their home debut, and it delayed by an hour the unveiling—a narrow 57-55 defeat by the Chicago Stags. The Green would lose their first five games and 10 of their first 11 en route to a 22-38 last-place tie in the Eastern Division of the new Basketball Association of America.

"We weren't much of a basketball team," Connors, Hollywood's future "Rifleman," would recall of that first Celtics team with a starting five averaging 6-feet-1 1/2 inches. "We were the *worst*."

Home attendance mirrored Celtics performance as "crowds" averaged 3,608. That translated into a $125,000 deficit, and the question was how long founder Walter Brown's baby would survive.

It was more of the same in 1947–48—another failing season at the box office and on the court—despite the 20-28 Celtics now featuring their first major scorer and all-leaguer. Big Ed Sadowski succeeded Connors in the pivot, and his 19.4-point average was the league's third best. And the Celts made the play-offs for the first time before being wiped out quickly, losing two of their three games.

After two feeble seasons, John "Honey" Russell was out as coach, replaced by Holy Cross's Alvin "Doggie" Julian. And after two more dismal years—missing the playoffs both seasons—Julian was through, too.

So were Boston Garden-Arena Corporation stockholders when Celtic red ink approached

John "Honey" Russell

$500,000. Brown, the group's president who also headed its Bruins and Celtics properties, was told to give up on a bad investment. They dumped the Celts, selling them to Brown, who hocked his home and drained savings to keep the team alive. And he brought in Providence sportsman Lou Pieri as a partner to help shoulder the financial burden.

Brown promptly spent $10,000 on a new coach, a brash 32-year-old cigar-smoker named Arnold Auerbach. Walter never made a better investment. "Red" Auerbach not only turned the Celtics around, he created the greatest team in basketball history—becoming a Boston institution in the process.

Auerbach got off to a rocky start at his welcoming press luncheon. He quickly got everyone's attention by insulting a local idol named Bob Cousy. Although the Celtics would soon land the flashy Holy Cross playmaker, they ignored The Cooz in the draft—opting for 7-foot Charlie Share as the big man to rebuild around. Passing over Cousy dumbfounded and angered New Englanders. When pressed for Celtics reasoning by the press at his coming-out party, Auerbach gave a preview of often-stormy coming attractions. "Walter," Red snapped impatiently, turning in irritation to Brown, "am I supposed to win or am I supposed to worry about the local yokels and please these guys?"

The Celtics' fortunes improved on the collapse of two other franchises. Cousy became a Celtic in a lottery distributing the talent of Chicago's folded team. And pivotman Ed Macauley was acquired when St. Louis failed. Cousy and Macauley became cornerstones on which Auerbach built his Celtics.

*O*wner Walter Brown shakes the hand of Bob Cousy during a meeting with the 1953–54 Celtics. Front row, from left, are Bob Harris, Ed Macauley, Bob Brannum, Cousy, and Bill Sharman. Chuck Cooper, Ernie Barrett, Bob Donham, and Ed Mikan are in the back row.

It was during the 1950 draft that Brown opened the second round by selecting All-American Chuck Cooper of Duquesne—the first Black player drafted in the rechristened National Basketball Association.

The transformed Celtics were on their way. Auerbach's first Boston team was the first to post a winning record, 39-30. And before the 1951–52 campaign, Auerbach talked Bill Sharman out of Dodger blue and into Celtics green. The fiery sharpshooter was an ideal backcourt partner for Cousy, and they combined with Macauley as the Big Three that would make the Celts an exciting fastbreak team into the mid-fifties—but a contender that fell short every spring.

By 1956, Auerbach had added more key ingredients to his mix—Frank Ramsey, Jungle Jim Loscutoff, and soon-to-be Rookie of the Year Tom Heinsohn. One missing link remained, and it arrived at Christmastime, when Bill Russell strolled onto the parquet directly from Australia, where he and a pal named K. C. Jones had led the USA to Olympic gold.

Russell signed for $19,500 and quickly proved worth every penny as a dominating center who introduced an awesome defensive dimension to the position. "Russ revolutionized basketball and was the man who made us go," Cousy said. "Without him we wouldn't have won a championship."

The first loomed ahead. The 1956–57 Celtics were in first place at 16-8 when Russell arrived, and now there was no catching them while breezing to a best-in-league 44-28 and their first division crown by six games over old nemesis

*T*he early Celtics were a portrait of futility and frustration. Consider one particularly Fellini-like nightmare in St. Louis.

An eager Celtic substitute checking into the game became confused and reported to a broadcaster at courtside instead of the scorer, earning a technical foul. The foul shot was made, a point that would loom large by game's end. The Green would lose by one point. Of course.

Despite that mistake, the Celts had appeared headed for victory—until blowing a six-point lead in the final half minute as coach Honey Russell flirted with cardiac arrest.

"That was one of our more imaginative and frustrating losses," Russell would recall. "I called a time-out with 26 seconds left and said, 'OK, boys, you know the situation: We have the ball and a six-point lead. The only way we can lose is for (Chuck) Connors to get the ball.'

"Everyone in the huddle started laughing, and I said I was serious.

"So we take the ball out under the St. Louis basket, and what happens? All four of my men on the floor drop back and the pass-in is weak. It's intercepted for a quick basket.

"Now we're up by four points with 23 seconds left. We manage to put the ball in play to one of our own guys this time and pass it around a few times before it's stolen. Swish! Now we're ahead by two points with about 10 seconds left and no time-outs. We have the ball. St. Louis is really pressing now and there's only one of our people open—Chuck Connors.

"So the pass goes to him and he starts dribbling with that high dribble of his. Then he trips, loses the ball, and grabs the leg of the St. Louis player who has recovered the ball and is tossing up a desperation shot to beat the clock.

"As the ball goes through the hoop to tie the game, the referee calls the foul on Connors. St. Louis makes the free throw and we lose.

"Mad? I fined Connors $200 on the spot, but it wasn't his fault," said Russell, "Chuck just did what came natural to him—he loused up."

BOB COUSY'S HEROICS

Bob Cousy lofts a shot over Cincinnati's befuddled defenders during the 1963 playoffs.

Four decades later, it remains etched in basketball legend, one of the classic games in NBA history—a wild playoff megathriller that solidified acceptance of the Celtics in Boston.

Saturday afternoon, March 21, 1953, at Boston Garden: Celtics 111, Syracuse Nationals 105 in *four* overtime periods. In a heroic performance, Bob Cousy scored 50 points while playing 66 of the marathon's 68 minutes despite a thigh pull that had him limping. Making Cousy's spree all the more spectacular was that they were 50 *pressure* points. The 24-year-old Celt sparkplug converted 30 of 32 free throws, including 18 in a row, and 25 of his points came in overtime with the game on the line.

"Nobody who saw that game will forget the game or Cooz," recalls Red Auerbach, then in his third season coaching the Celtics. "He was fabulous, just fabulous."

Watching in wide-eyed wonder were 11,058 spectators, who by game's end were drained from an emotional roller coaster that had transported them through three hours and eleven minutes of melodramatic peaks and valleys. It was a game that Jack Barry reported in the next morning's *Boston Globe* as "defying description."

The delirium began early. Fisticuffs between Syracuse's Dolph Schayes and Boston's Bob Brannum not far into the second period nearly ignited a riot as Nats Paul Seymour and Billy Gabor challenged a squad of Boston Police who had come onto the floor. The frenzy continued throughout the game as the lead swung back and forth like a pendulum as the Garden rocked.

Fourteen of the game's 20 players were disqualified—12 fouled out, Brannum and Schayes thrown out. But three disqualified Nats and one disqualified Celtic were allowed to stay in the game so each team could field five players. Referees awarded an extra free throw when a disqualified player committed a foul.

The quadruple-overtime hysteria proved too much for two Celtics officials, a pair who had been with the team since its birth—in fact, who had collaborated to name the club. Midway through those frantic overtimes, publicist Howie McHugh was overcome by headaches so severe that he passed out in the pressbox. And elsewhere in the Garden, Walter Brown, his chest throbbing, left his seat and paced the lobby for the remainder of the game. But the Celtics founder could not escape the roar of the crowd, and it lured him to frequently peek through a firedoor to check the big scoreboard suspended over midcourt. One shot after another. An eight-column banner headline splashing across the next day's *Globe* told it all, proclaiming:

"Cousy Does Everything in Victory but Take Tickets."

Years later Bob Cousy reminisces: "No game is more memorable for me than that one."

Syracuse. And the Green continued to roll in the playoffs, wiping out the Nats in three straight before wrapping up the championship trophy against St. Louis.

"We've been trying to get to the top for seven years, and we're finally here," said Cousy, the NBA's Most Valuable Player.

The Celtics fell short in 1957–58. The regular season wasn't a problem. The Celtics won five more games than the previous season (49), collected a second straight East title and routed a good Philadelphia team 4-1 in the division finals.

Disaster struck in the third minute of the third period of the third game of the championship rematch against the Hawks in St. Louis. With the series tied at a victory apiece, Russell, the NBA's MVP, soared to block a Bob Pettit shot—and landed heavily on his left foot, the ankle buckling beneath him as he crashed to the floor in a heap.

The ankle was severely sprained, and included a chip fracture. Russ was essentially through for the series and the Celtics would soon be dethroned. Russell tried to play, discarding crutches for Game 6 as Boston faced elimination. But he was only a shadow of himself as the Celtics were counted out, 110-109. Now a Hawk, Ed Macauley would note: "If Russell hadn't been hurt, we wouldn't have beaten the Celtics." And in the Boston locker room, Auerbach put a hand on Russell's shoulder and whispered: "There will be other seasons, Russ."

And other championships—eight in a row. Count 'em, *eight*. Even the cocky Auerbach—who would coach until 1966 and never again taste championship defeat—couldn't have dreamed such a procession would follow.

A deposed champion with something to prove, the Celtics raced through the 1958–59 schedule in a runaway, a scoring machine shredding NBA records along the way. And none was more flabbergasting than a 173-139 bombing of the Lakers. A Garden crowd of 6,183 was agog at the display of awesome offense (headed by Heinsohn's 43 points and Cousy's 28 assists) and awkward defense as the Celtics shattered a half dozen NBA scoring records. The barrage stunned everyone, including Auerbach, who said, "I've never seen anything like it."

The Celtics went on to set a league record for most victories (52-20), while winning the division by a dozen games. And after finally subduing Syracuse in seven-game drama in the Eastern Finals, the Celts reclaimed their crown by blitzing the Lakers in four straight—the first championship series sweep ever, an exclamation mark to a season-long statement.

It was much of the same in 1959–60—only more so. While rookie Wilt Chamberlain was dominating statistics around the league, the Celtics were ruling the victory column. They won 11 of their first 12 games before stringing together a 17-victory streak that left them 30-4 by New Year's—rolling to an NBA record 59-16 finish, 10 games ahead of Wilt's Warriors. The Celtics vanquished the Warriors in six in the playoffs, then defeated the Hawks in seven—retaining the championship with an emphatic 19-point victory in the clincher, Russell devastating with 35 rebounds and 22 points. "He played one of the truly great games of all time," Bob Pettit toasted his rival superstar. "He never did anything wrong."

Nor did he for at least the next three seasons apparently as Russell swept three consecutive NBA MVP trophies while the Celtics' beat stroked on: another spring, another championship.

There was a changing of the guard after the Celts rang up their third and fourth straight titles in 1961 and '62. Sharman departed, replaced by Sam Jones—one sharpshooter succeeding another. Sam had been groomed for this opportunity, brought along slowly—just as was the other Jones,

The Celtics made history in 1950 when they selected Chuck Cooper, the first Black drafted in the NBA. The Duquesne star, a 6-foot-5 forward, went on to play four seasons with Boston, averaging 6.8 points and 6.6 rebounds, his place in history secure. "Walter Brown was the man who put his neck on the line," Cooper would look back decades later. "It took a lot of guts. He was a gentleman of backbone and made it possible when nobody else would."

K. C., who would fill the other backcourt slot when Cousy retired.

TOM HEINSOHN ON WILT:

Not only was I Red Auerbach's whipping boy, but he damn near got me killed by Wilt Chamberlain. Red had me pester Wilt in a way just about guaranteed to infuriate Chamberlain. And it did infuriate him. And when it did, Wilt threatened to tear me apart, and damn near did.

First, you've got to understand that Wilt Chamberlain was the world's strongest man, King Kong in sneakers. He claimed to be 7-foot-1, 250 pounds, but looked a lot bigger to me. And he was powerful. The man was capable of dribbling me, and stuffing me through a hoop. As a rookie, the strategy around the league was to foul him when he got the ball inside. Wilt was deadly around the basket, but a poor foul shooter. I was the lucky Celtic grabbing him most often, and so Wilt and I got to know each other quite well his first season. A fight started one night in Philadelphia, and for some reason Chamberlain went after me. He grabbed me by my shoulder straps and ripped himself a handful of uniform like nothing at all. Well, that gave me a hint that Wilt's patience was wearing thin.

Another tactic the Celtics used against Wilt then was something to exploit his slowness in making the transition from offense to defense. After Philly foul shots, we got a lot of fastbreak baskets by Russell outhustling Chamberlain back up the floor, taking a long pass from Cousy, and stuffing for two easy points. We'd get as many as 10 points a game doing this, and we did it all season. Wilt started catching on, of course, so Auerbach decided to add a wrinkle in the playoffs. He wanted someone to get in Chamberlain's way, a human stumbling block to impede him as we started up court. The idea was to step in front of Wilt and cut him off while Russell took off with a nice head start. There were no volunteers, of course. Who in his right mind wants to step in front of a subway train? And when nobody stepped up, naturally Red volunteered me. 'You're it, Heinsohn.' Of course."

The lightning-quick Sam and another galloping new starter, Tom Sanders (taking over the opposite corner from Heinsohn), renewed team speed as the Celtics raced to their record fourth-in-a-row championship.

A heady 60-20 while sprinting to the Eastern title by 11 games, the Celtics had to gut out their toughest playoffs yet—14 memorable thrillers as Boston survived stern tests by Philadelphia and Los Angeles. Each Game 7 hung on a desperate, agonizing shot with two seconds left on the Garden clock—and both spelled Boston victory. Thank you, Sam Jones (whose 18-foot fallaway beat the Sixers). And thank you, Frank Selvy (whose missed shot skidded off the rim and sank the Lakers).

A different strain of emotion gripped the Garden in 1962–63. From beginning to end, it was the Year of The Cooz—Bob Cousy's last hurrah. And the team won it all for their captain.

First the Celtics danced to the east title by a 10-victory margin over Syracuse. And before the "Houdini of the Hardwood" retired to coach at Boston College, the 34-year-old Cousy had a few playoff thrills to dispense—saving one final heroic for the end. As the Celts struggled to close out Game 6 at Los Angeles, in a touch worthy of Hollywood, Cooz limped off the bench on a severely sprained ankle and dribbled out the clock before heaving the ball to the rafters as the buzzer ended an era.

Cousy gone, the Celtics had to prove they could win in 1963–64 without him—and did, winning one more game, 59, as though to prove it. The Celtics also introduced a new pressing defense, made relentless by ballhawking Russell, Sanders, K. C. Jones, and a perpetual-motion sophomore named John Havlicek. He was succeeding Ramsey as the NBA's premier sixth man as Frank played a final season. Although never starting, Hondo led team scoring with a 19.9-point average off the fastbreak quarterbacked by K. C., who dealt out the third most assists in the league.

It all added up to another East title before the Celtics romped through the playoffs in five-game sets over the Oscar Robertson/Jerry Lucas Royals and Wilt-led Warriors. Now it was Ramsey's and Loscutoff's turn to go out winners as the Celts became the first pro team to win six successive world championships—surpassing the five straight collected by baseball's 1949–53 Yankees and hockey's 1956–60 Canadiens.

It also proved 59-year-old Walter Brown's final championship. A week before 1964 training camp opened, he suffered a fatal heart attack at his Cape Cod retreat. And when No. 1 was retired for the Celtics' founder on opening night, Russell vowed: "We'll win the championship for Mr. Brown's memory."

And they did, thanks to some crucial thievery. Otherwise, instead of being forever known as the Year Havlicek Stole the Ball, it might have been the Season the Celtics Blew It. They made a shambles of their division, jumping to a 31-7 start by New Year's and surpassing their own NBA record

for most victories, winning 62 while losing only 18, to ring up their ninth consecutive east pennant by 14 games.

The sizzling Eastern playoffs followed as Boston and Philadelphia split six games, each rival winning before rabid homefolk

Bill Russell's All-Star uniform

Sam Jones was a premier shooting guard before the game had such a title. "Sudden Sam" played a key role in 10 Celtics championships and averaged 17.7 points a game over a 12-year career to earn berths on both the NBA's Silver Anniversary team and in the Hall of Fame. Quick afoot and deadly accurate, Jones' bank shots are a part of Celtics lore.

FOLLOWING SPREAD:

It will always be remembered as one of the classic head-to-head matchups in NBA history—Bill Russell vs. Wilt Chamberlain. Chamberlain was taller and stronger, and through their confrontations the dominant scorer. But the quicker Russell's defense, rebounding, and floor play usually tipped the scales in favor of the Celtics.

who frequently rained eggs on the enemy. But the biggest egg was laid by an unlikely source—Bill Russell, when his pass-in struck the guy wire as the Garden clock clicked off the final seconds of Game 7. That's when Havlicek stole the ball, promoting the Celtics to the championship round. Los Angeles proved no competition without Elgin Baylor, who watched helplessly with torn knee ligaments while the Celtics trampled the Lakers.

"This was Walter Brown's championship," Auerbach said after his victory shower, displaying the late owner's St. Christopher medal, which the coach had secretly carried with him every game that season. "We won it for him."

Before the 1965–66 season, the 48-year-old Auerbach announced he would coach one last year before retiring from the bench to concentrate on general managing. He was giving ample notice so enemies "can take one last shot at me" as the Celtics took aim at an eighth-straight NBA championship in his 20th and final season coaching in the league.

For the first time in 10 seasons, Boston didn't win the regular-season title in the East, finishing a game behind the 55-25 Sixers, who won their last 11. That meant Boston didn't get its usual first-round bye, but prevailed anyway over Cincinnati, Philadelphia, and Los Angeles—and at the end survived that near backfiring of Auerbach's final victory cigar.

Red went out a winner. But there would be no championship in the Celtics first season without their old mentor courtside in 1966–67, the Year the Greatest Sports Dynasty Ended. It was Philadelphia's season as Chamberlain finally emerged a winner after seven frustrating seasons of being foiled by archrival Russell.

It was also the year the Celtics broke another color line. They had drafted and signed the first Black in NBA history. They had been the first to start five Blacks. Now they became the first team in *any* major league sport to be directed by a Black as Auerbach handed over the reins to Russell. Player-coach Russell led the Celtics to 60 victories, six more than the previous season and matching the second-most ever by a Celtics team. Yet

As a basketball player, John Havlicek was omnipresent. If he didn't have the ball, he was chasing it or racing into position to receive it. He played forward and guard, but his real position was athlete. His key statistics, eight world titles and more than 30,000 points in both regular-season and playoff games—are the only way to look at Hondo's career.

incredibly, that 60-21 record left Boston eight games behind the 76ers, whose 68-13 easily eclipsed the NBA's previous best of 62-18 by the '64-'65 Celtics.

Still, the Celtics had a 5-4 advantage in their season series, reason for optimism among Boston fans despite knowing their team was aging. Russell was 33, Sam nearly 34, and K. C. almost 35 as he prepared to retire.

It was like old times as the Celtics rolled over the Knicks, 3-2, in the playoffs' opening round. But the East finals against the Sixers were another story. The Celtics won only one game, the fourth, avoiding the indignity of a sweep. When the Sixers buried Boston, 140-116, to end it, Convention Hall rocked to "Boston is dead! . . . Boston is dead!" As the buzzer ended the reign, Russell put an arm around K. C. and they walked off a basketball floor as teammates for the last time—ending a trail that had taken them from NCAA championships to Olympic gold to a string of NBA crowns.

K. C. was the only hero of the Dynasty Celtics to go out a loser. A *loser*—that was a strange label for the Celtics. And it would only be temporary, Havlicek assured teammates at the club's breakup dinner the following night, announcing, "We're only dead until October."

The Celtics launched the 1967–68 season with six victories in a row and by Christmas were 25-7. But the Sixers were rolling, too, and by schedule's end were 62-20, eight wins better than Boston, in second place for the third straight season.

And after getting by Detroit in the playoff opener, the Celtics fell into a 1-3 hole against Philadelphia. It seemed an impossible task for the old, tired, and bruised Celts to beat the mighty Sixers three straight, especially with two of those games scheduled for the new Spectrum. But they did—and then KO'd the Lakers in six.

So for the 10th time in 12 years, the Celtics were world champions. Their dynasty wasn't over after all, just interrupted briefly.

Make that 11 championships in 13 seasons as the Celtics won again in 1968–69—rebounding from *fourth* place, their lowest finish in 20 years, nine games off the top.

Clearly, the Celtics had gotten old. Sam Jones, who had announced he'd retire at season's end, was the oldest player in the league at nearly 36. Russell, who had been mulling retirement for some time, was 35. The average age of the Celtics eight regulars was a creaky 31. The Celtics were over the hill, many felt. Yes, there had been a plaguing rash of injuries all season, but wasn't that a symptom of old age?

Meanwhile, the Lakers had beefed up their lineup by adding old friend Wilt to the team with Baylor and West, a Big Three that had Los Angeles planning a coronation as part of what some called the "greatest team ever assembled." Boston would see about that. After disposing of Philadelphia and New York in the playoffs, the Celtics entered the finals as underdog defending champions. The showdown went the seven-game route before the Celtics won at the end, Don Nelson's desperate off-balance 15-footer proving decisive.

Of the Celtics' 11 NBA championships, this was the sweetest—gutted out after being written off as has-beens. It was a triumph to savor— and would have to last for a while. Sam Jones retired. So did Russell. And the defending champs would undergo an overhaul under a new coach named Heinsohn, who would rebuild the Celtics. But first, the Celtics sank to the bottom in 1969–70, suffering their first losing season (34-48) in two decades. But Heinsohn built for the future by playing the youngsters—most notably rookie Jo Jo White and sophomore Don Chaney in the backcourt.

Don Nelson played forward with a calculated passion that later made him a successful NBA coach. Neither a dominant scorer or rebounder, the 6-foot-6 Nelson played both ends of the court with a clever tenacity that wore opponents down during his 11 Celtic seasons.

There was another silver lining. The Celtics had their best drafting position in 16 years. Selecting fourth, the Celtics got the center they wanted—Dave Cowens, the rugged man in the middle so desperately needed.

Cowens was clearly a Celtics-type who would improve the club. The only question: was the 6-foot-8 1/2 dynamo big enough to play the NBA pivot. Or would he be a forward? That's where Cowens started his first few games as a Celt before being shifted to center, which he preferred—and where he'd prove so pivotal to the Celtics' future.

With young Cowens, the Celtics were improved but consistently inconsistent while suffering more growing pains during a 44-38 season in 1970–71. The erratic play left Havlicek, the captain and glue who held the team together (while averaging a still-best-ever 28.9 points while playing over 45 minutes a game) fuming at one point: "This is the dumbest team I ever played on."

There would be no sophomore letdown for Cowens in 1971–72. Co-Rookie of the Year the previous season, he became the East's starting center in the All-Star Game. And Boston was winning more—posting its best record (56-26) in five years and its first division title since 1965. While often starting four players under age 25, the Celtics out-distanced New York by eight games. But a season of uppers ended on a downer as the young Celtics were wiped out in five games by the Knicks in the conference finals. The renaissance still needed work—and a power forward to help Cowens on the boards and stand watch underneath when Dave was roaming.

Welcome, Paul Silas. He arrived from Phoenix in another Auerbach master stroke—in exchange for rights to a player the Celtics never had, Charlie Scott. Silas proved exactly the right final ingredient in the Celtics' victory soup—a

Two of the most dominant centers of the 1970s, Dave Cowens and Bill Walton, then of Portland, battled for rebounding position. Although Walton was at least 2 1/2-inches taller than Cowens, the pair emphasized the same strengths in their games—court savvy, quickness, positioning, defense, and desire. Eventually, both would play key roles in Celtics championships. Cowens led Boston to two titles in 1973–74 and 1975–76. Walton finished his career in Boston and played a pivotal role in the 1986 title after being named the NBA's best sixth man.

banger who brought eight-season experience and 6-foot-7, 220-pound brawn to help Cowens patrol inside. The 1972–73 edition was the best Celtics team that didn't win a championship. With Cowens having an MVP season, and Heinsohn Coach of the Year, the Celtics forged their best record ever, 68-14, and finished 11 games ahead of New York.

The Celtics and Knicks met again in the Eastern Conference finals. With the series tied, Havlicek wrecked a shoulder while fighting through a pick in Game 3. Without Havlicek, the Celtics blew a 16-point lead in the final 10 minutes before losing Game 4 in double-overtime at New York. Down 1-3, Havlicek returned valiantly as a one-armed superstar often shooting left-handed as he helped tie the series with two heroic wins. The Celtics had never lost a seventh game, but did now, going flat before home fans as the Knicks exploited the wounded Havlicek to win easily—before moving on to seize the NBA championship by dethroning the Lakers.

"We would have won the championship if I hadn't hurt my shoulder," Havlicek would say over the years. "I'm sure of it."

And the next season they did. After starting out 29-6, the Celtics played little better than win-one-lose-one basketball from then on. Last season's zest seemed gone as the team lurched to another division title at 56-26, a dozen fewer wins—not encouraging for the playoffs ahead.

So it was something of a surprise when the Celtics marched through Buffalo, New York City, and Milwaukee to the title as Havlicek celebrated his 34th birthday as the finals' MVP.

It was the Celtics' 12th world championship, but this reign lasted one day short of a year. It had taken the Celts five years to regain the NBA crown, and it took K. C. Jones' Washington Bullets six games to wrench it away.

It was a stunning climax to a 1974–75 season in which the Celts won 60 games, dominated the Atlantic Division by 11 games and demolished the Houston Rockets in five games in the playoffs' opening round. And then they met their match, both competitively and stylistically. Old favorite K. C. had molded a team that featured a running game and clutching face-to-face defense similar to the style he had practiced as a Celtic. "Playing them," Havlicek said of Elvin Hayes, Wes Unseld, Phil Chenier, and the other Bullets, "is like looking in the mirror."

The Celtics regained their throne the following spring in a finals featuring that wild triple-overtime classic at the Garden. Finals MVP Jo Jo White contributed 33 points to that 128-126 thriller which gave Boston a 3-2 edge over the Suns and put the Celts on the threshold of their 13th NBA championship two days later.

The Celtics had appeared a team in transition that season, going through another changing of the guard. Don Chaney had departed for the ABA and Auerbach replaced him by trading third-guard Paul Westphal to Phoenix for Charlie Scott—the same Scott whose rights Red had dealt to Phoenix for Paul Silas. There were concerns that because Scott and White were both shooters they wouldn't be compatible in the backcourt. But Scott adjusted from bombardier to multipurpose guard and the pair teamed well. So did Havlicek, Cowens, and Silas upfront. That veteran trio was named first-team all-defense—an achievement that's never been duplicated.

Bill Fitch and Larry Bird both arrived in Boston for the 1979–80 season. Bird was named Rookie of the Year. Fitch was named Coach of the Year. A season later, Kevin McHale and Robert Parish came along and Fitch coached Boston to the first championship of the Celtics' golden eighties.

The 1976 Championship ended a Celtics era. Nelson retired. Silas, bogged down in a salary impasse, was traded to Denver. And eight games into the 1976–77 season, Cowens was gone, too—saying he'd lost his enthusiasm and was taking an "indefinite leave of absence." As suddenly as he'd disappeared, Cowens returned after a 30-game absence. And less than a minute into Cowens' first game back, Scott fractured a forearm. But behind a remotivated Cowens, Boston went on to win 41 games and take second place behind Philadelphia, who would eliminate the Celts in seven games in the Eastern semifinals.

The 1977–78 season was worse. On paper it had appeared a remarkable collection of talent—seven had played in at least one All-Star Game and three seemed destined for the Hall of Fame. There was Cowens in the pivot, old UCLA soulmates Wicks and Curtis Rowe in the corners, White and Scott in the backcourt. Dave Bing was signed as a third guard. And Havlicek, approaching his 38th birthday, was back in his sixth-man role. Yet no Celtic team had ever played with less cohesion and less spirit, heard more catcalls from fans—or finished with a worse record, 32-50.

When the season was over, Heinsohn had been fired (replaced at midseason by assistant Tom Sanders), Scott traded (for the returning Chaney), Havlicek retired, and the Celtics had missed the playoffs for the first time since 1971.

Before his career finale, Havlicek told Sanders: "I began my career running and I want to end it running for all 48 minutes." Hondo settled for 41, and wept when Sanders took him out with 15 seconds remaining—after contributing 29 points in his 1,270th Celtics game, an NBA record for longevity.

For those who thought 1977–78 had been a nightmare, 1978–79 would be worse—spelled b-i-z-a-r-r-e.

For openers, the Celtics were *traded*. Owner Irv Levin and Buffalo counterpart John Y. Brown played musical franchises and swapped teams. Brown would keep the Celts in Boston while Levin moved the Braves to San Diego and renamed them the Clippers. Adding to the dizziness, the exchange included a megatrade as Boston bundled off four players including Wicks for Tiny Archibald, Marvin Barnes, and Billy Knight.

Auerbach had dealt with an assortment of team ownerships during the 15 years since Walter Brown's death, but this shift jolted him to consider leaving after nearly three decades at the helm. At age 60 he didn't need this. So Red met with the Knicks after they reportedly teased with the highest salary ever offered an NBA executive. And on the parquet, a revolving door was spinning as 18 players wore Celtics Green. Jo Jo White and Dennis Awtrey were traded for first-round draft picks. After 28 games, Barnes was waived. Chris Ford and Rick Robey arrived in trades. So did Bob McAdoo, who came from the Knicks for three first-round draft choices Auerbach had been saving. "I was afraid maybe I'd pick up the paper one day and find out *I* was traded," Auerbach told the *Boston Globe*.

A victim of the chaos was the coach. After the team lost 12 of their first 14 games, Tom Sanders was dismissed after less than a year on the job and Cowens was made player-coach. "There was turmoil in the front office," recalled Cowens, who'd retire as coach at season's end but remain as a player. "Nobody knew what was going on. And with most of our veterans gone, we were almost like an expansion club."

Predictably, the Celtics suffered through their worst season, skidding to the pits with their poorest

Guards Nate "Tiny" Archibald, below, and Danny Ainge, facing page, played important roles in championship drives. A quick, penetrating point guard, Archibald turned in his best games as a Celtic during the championship run of '81, averaging 15.6 points and 6.3 assists in the playoffs. An instigator who stirred emotions and the offense the second he came on the floor, the fiery Ainge—who was also a deadly accurate shooter from beyond the three-point line—shot 55 percent from the floor, made 41 steals and averaged a career playoff high of 15.6 points in '86 to help the Celtics to a second title in three seasons.

Robert Parish's number hasn't been retired yet, but the Chief's distinctive "00" has earned its place in Celtics history. Every Celtics championship team was anchored by a strong presence in the middle. The Celtics of Bill Russell won 11 titles. The Celtics of Dave Cowens won two. Parish arrived in Boston on June 9, 1980, as part of one of the most significant trades in Celtics history. The Celtics swapped their No. 1 overall spot in the draft to Golden State for Parish and the draft's No. 3 pick (Kevin McHale). The rest is history. Larry Bird, Parish and McHale formed the Celtics' "Big Three" upfront that helped win three more championships in the '80s. For more than a decade, Bird and McHale flanked Parish. The forwards garnered more awards, but couldn't have done it without the presence of the 7-foot 1/2-inch, 230-pound Parish in the middle. He played in nine NBA All-Star Games and was twice named All-NBA. Parish played 14 seasons with Boston. In the Celtics' career rankings, Parish ranks second in games (1,106), third in points (18,245), second in rebounds (11,051) and third in field-goal percentage (.552). When he departed for Charlotte after the 1993–94 season, Parish was the oldest player in the NBA at 40. Of Parish, Bird once said: "Chief is our rock in the middle. He gives us the freedom to do what we do best."

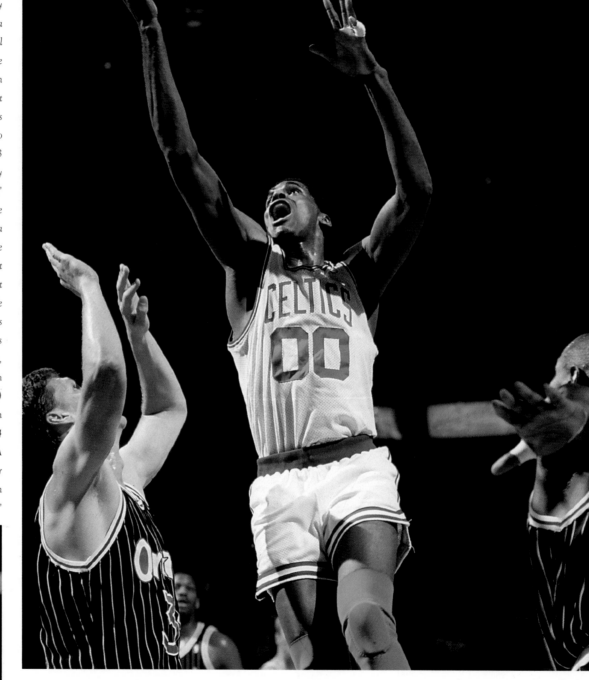

record ever, a feeble 29-53. It meant the club's first last-place finish in 29 years. But there was one super silver lining.

Before the owner swap, Auerbach maneuvered a gamble that would rate with the Bill Russell acquisition. Using the sixth overall pick in the draft, the Celtics selected Larry Bird. Every NBA general manager hungered for the 6-foot-9 prodigy forward, but few would wait a year for delivery. Nor did they want the risk; if Bird weren't signed within a year, the drafter's rights would expire.

After a year of speculation, the college Player of the Year proved worth the wait—and the money, reportedly $3.25 million over five years that made him the highest-paid rookie in sports history. Bird wasn't the only newcomer participating in the 1979–80 renewal. There was a new owner, Harry Mangurian, buying out partner John Y. Brown, who'd gone off to become governor of Kentucky. There was a new coach, Bill Fitch, who'd been Coach of the Year with Cleveland. And there were five new players in all.

It added up to a revamped team attitude, a return to the Celtics way. Boston improved by 32 victories to win the Atlantic title by two games over Philadelphia with a best-in-league 61-21. That equaled the number of Celtics wins mustered in the previous two seasons combined.

From the start, Bird was never a rookie despite what it said on his Rookie of the Year trophy. He led the club in minutes (averaging 36 a game), points (21.6), rebounds (10.4), and steals (1.7), and dished out more assists (4.5) than any Celtic but playmaker Tiny Archibald (8.4). But after sweeping the Rockets in the playoffs' opening round, the Celtics were ousted in five games by Julius Erving and the Sixers. While a disappointing finish, it had been an extraordinary season.

And 1980–81 would be better—four months before it began. Auerbach and Fitch walked into the June draft with the No. 1 pick and cashed it in for *two* giants who would help shape the Celtics' distinctive look for a dozen years.

The Celtics, victim on draft day was Golden State, which wanted the No. 1 pick to corral Joe Barry Carroll. In exchange, the Celtics got 7-foot 1/2-inch center Robert Parish plus the Warriors' No. 3 choice, used to take 6-foot-10 Kevin McHale of Minnesota. In one artful master stroke, Boston's smallish frontline was transformed into one of the NBA's bigger and more versatile fronts. These Celtics could even cope with Cowens' sudden retirement during the preseason as the 62-20 Green had a blend and cohesion that transported them to the NBA title, a reborn team that in two years had gone from laughing stock to champion.

The 1981–82 Celtics set a goal of becoming the first team to repeat as champions since the 1969 team. They met the challenge during the regular season by assembling a 63-29 record, best in the league. While capturing a third straight Atlantic title, the Celtics never lost more than two consecutive games and strung together a club record 18-victory streak, part of a late surge in which they won 25 of their last 29 games.

Along the way the Celtics landed another in court when Auerbach coaxed All-American guard/infielder Danny Ainge from baseball's Toronto Blue Jays. The Celtics settled with the Jays for a reported $800,000—money well spent when measured by the eight spirited seasons Ainge gave Boston.

Washington proved a stubborn and physical foe in the playoffs' opening round, 3-1. Bostonians then had visions of Philadelphia being a stepping stone to the title round for the second straight spring, particularly after the Celtics won Game 1 by 40 points at the Garden, a 121-81 blitz called the Mother's Day Massacre. But the Sixers had other ideas and won the next three to put the Celtics on the brink—and without sparkplug Tiny Archibald, who dislocated a shoulder diving for a loose ball in Game 3. The Celtics battled back to tie the series at 3-3. That's when Philadelphia did

S*trong center play is a Celtics tradition that began with Bill Russell and continued with Dave Cowens. Robert Parish, left, and Bill Walton, shown below hooking home two over the Bulls' Michael Jordan, gave the Celtics a potent 1-2 punch in the middle during the championship campaign of 1985–86. The Chiefs' distinctive "00" was a fixture in the middle throughout the '80s. Walton joined the Celtics for the 1985–86 season and was named the NBA's top sixth man before recurring ankle and foot injuries ended his career a year later. Together, Parish and Walton neutralized Houston's Akeem Olajuwon and Ralph Sampson in the 1986 championship series.*

something it had never done before—win a seventh-game showdown at Boston. The Celtics were *former* champs again.

The Sixers only got tougher in 1982–83. Adding Moses Malone, they won 65 to run off with the division and sailed to the NBA championship. Despite 56 wins, the Celtics finished nine games behind in the Atlantic, and matters got worse in the postseason. After squeezing by Atlanta, 2-1, they were wiped out by the Milwaukee Bucks—the only time the Celtics ever were swept in a best-of-seven series.

Bill Fitch soon resigned, replaced by assistant K. C. Jones. And in further stunning news, Auerbach made one of his more larcenous deals by shipping backup Rick Robey to Phoenix for All-Star guard Dennis Johnson, who would be the Celtics' playmaker/ballhawking defender for seasons to come. All the parts were falling into place.

The 1983–84 Celtics went 62-20, won their division by 10 games and raced to Championship Banner 15, clinching against the Lakers in Game 7 at the Garden on June 12: Flag Day.

Like the league's other 14 consecutive one-year champions since 1969, the 1984–85 Green couldn't repeat. But it wasn't from lack of trying. The Celts again went to the finals, this time falling short to an overdue rival.

Here was a Larry Bird idiosyncrasy that became part of Celtics folklore. Each time Larry went to the foul line, he'd wipe his hands across the soles of his shoes. Nervous twitch? Superstition? Keeping his shooting hand dry? All of the above? No one ever messed with the system, however. On top of everything else he brought to the floor, Bird is the most accurate free throw shooter in Celtics history (88.6 percent).

The Celtics had gone 63-19 to win the division with two off-the-bench veterans recast in starting roles, Ainge at guard and McHale upfront. The Celtics wanted to start stockpiling draft picks for the future, and with Ainge now clearly ready to start regularly, Henderson was traded to Seattle for a number one (that would go for Len Bias) during the preseason. And early into the schedule, McHale replaced Maxwell when a knee problem sidelined Cedric much of the season.

Throughout the season, Boston and Los Angeles were on a collision course as the league's two dominant teams with nearly identical records. The rivals had faced each other in eight previous finals, and the Celtics had won all eight showdowns. Maybe it was the law of averages. Perhaps an injured right index finger which seemed to affect Bird's shooting had something to do with it. Whatever the reasons, after the teams divided the finals' first four games, the Lakers prevailed in six. Finally.

Due to the brilliance of Bird, the spotlight often missed Kevin McHale. Peers, however, considered the 6-foot-10 McHale one of the league's top all-around players. Shown here scoring over Houston's Akeem Olajuwon in the 1986 championship, McHale is the No. 4 scorer and No. 6 rebounder in Celtics history and a six-time selection on the NBA's all-defensive team. McHale played in seven NBA All-Star Games. Following the 1986–87 season, McHale was named first-team All-NBA . . . at the forward opposite Bird.

The Celtics bounced back in 1985–86 with a powerhouse that Auerbach would describe as "one of the greatest, if not the greatest, team I've ever been associated with."

Jan Volk, starting his third season as general manager, hammered the final pieces into place with two Auerbachian master strokes before camp. Bolstering the bench, Volk traded for a pair of NBA veterans who long had yearned to be Celtics—Jerry Sichting from the Pacers (for Quinn Buckner) and Bill Walton from the Clippers (for Maxwell, a first-round draft pick and cash). Sichting proved a sure-shooting third-guard supporting Johnson and Ainge.

The result was arguably the greatest team in NBA history. The Celtics romped home 13 games ahead of the Knicks at 67-15, the second-best in team history (one win less than 1972–73). And that included 40-1 at home (after an early December defeat by Portland at the Garden, they didn't lose there again until a year and six days later—48 straight wins).

Bird again was MVP, joining Bill Russell and Wilt Chamberlain as the only three-in-a-row recipients of the award. Despite back and elbow problems, Larry was in the league's top 10 in five areas—including fourth in scoring (25.8) and seventh

D uring the National Anthem, Larry Bird would stand at attention, looking up to the Stars & Stripes hanging from the Boston Garden rafters . . . and beyond to the banner honoring Boston Bruins superstar Bobby Orr. As a youth, Bird idolized Orr for the verve he brought to his sport, hockey. Bird sought to capture that on the basketball court. He succeeded.

in rebounding (9.8), and he led the club in most statistics including assists and steals.

And in the playoffs, it took just 12 games, one over minimum, for the Celtics to rumble past the Bulls, Hawks, and Bucks and advance to the finals, where old coach Bill Fitch and his Rockets awaited. Six games later, K. C. Jones' Celts completed the NBA's best-ever total record, 82-18, and banked their 16th world championship in 30 years.

"That was the best Celtics team I've ever seen and I'd stack it up with any I've seen anywhere else," Bird would say years later. "It was a fun year. There is no feeling like that championship feeling."

The euphoria didn't last long. In a June like no other, a rollercoaster transported Celtics emotions from the heights to the depths. They had regained their crown on the 8th. On the 17th they got the prize they coveted in the draft, a potential franchise player who could carry them into the nineties. And on the 19th that superprospect was dead of cocaine-related cardiac arrest.

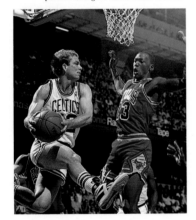

Jerry Sichting was a sure-shooting third-guard supporting Dennis Johnson and Danny Ainge. Sichting shot 57 percent in the 1985–86 championship season and 54 percent during his three Boston seasons.

Len Bias had been exactly what the Celts needed—a 6-foot-8 sharpshooting forward who would pump young blood into a lineup that was showing age. The tragedy clouded the start of the 1986–87 season, but despite an assortment of injuries the Celtics fought to the finals before falling short in their title defense.

The Celts won the division by 14 games as McHale enjoyed his best season despite a foot broken late. Kevin played with the hairline fracture through the playoffs as Boston swept past Chicago, 3-0, before outbattling Milwaukee and Detroit in seven-game thrillers. But the championship went to the Lakers in six games.

McHale's 1987–88 season was delayed while recuperating from off-season foot surgery, but Bird enjoyed his best scoring season at 29.9 as the Celtics won the Atlantic by 19—their eighth division title in nine years.

FOLLOWING SPREAD:

Here it is, the classic Celtics pick and roll. About to be burned are the Los Angeles Lakers. As Robert Parish sets a screen on Lakers forward James Worthy, Larry Bird breaks into a dribble toward the middle. And as Vlade Divac jumps out to block Bird's path to the basket, Larry lobs a return pass to the Chief, who burns Worthy for a textbook basket.

During the playoffs, K. C. Jones announced he would retire at season's end, replaced by assistant Jimmy Rodgers. Jones hoped to add another coaching ring before departing, but fell short. After ousting New York and Atlanta, the Celtics were stopped in six by Detroit (despite McHale's buzzer-beating three-pointer sending Game 2 into a second overtime period and an eventual Boston victory). K. C. headed upstairs with the best regular-season (.751) and playoff (.637) percentages of any Celtics coach.

Rodgers took over a 1988–89 team soon in transition. Bird would quickly be gone for the season (playing just six games before undergoing Achilles tendon surgery on both ankles). A silver lining was that sophomore Reggie Lewis, who had spent his rookie year mostly sitting and watching, stepped in just before his 23rd birthday and proved he could play in the NBA averaging 18.5 points. And in February, Ainge was traded to Sacramento, a move that pressed top draftee Brian Shaw into a backcourt tandem with DJ.

There was a cost to the transition. The Birdless Celts barely made it over .500 at 42-40 while tumbling to third place, 10 games out. A quick exit from the playoffs followed, swept 0-3 by eventual champion Detroit—the first time the Celtics had been first-round casualties since 1956.

The Celtics were KO'd in the first round again in 1989–90, even though Bird (and his 24.3 average) was back and the team improved to 52-30 while finishing just one game out of first. The Knicks were the executioners this time, seizing the deciding fifth game at Boston, and where they had lost 27 straight games dating back to 1984; the Knicks won the final three games of the best-of-five series. And with the Celts out, two days later

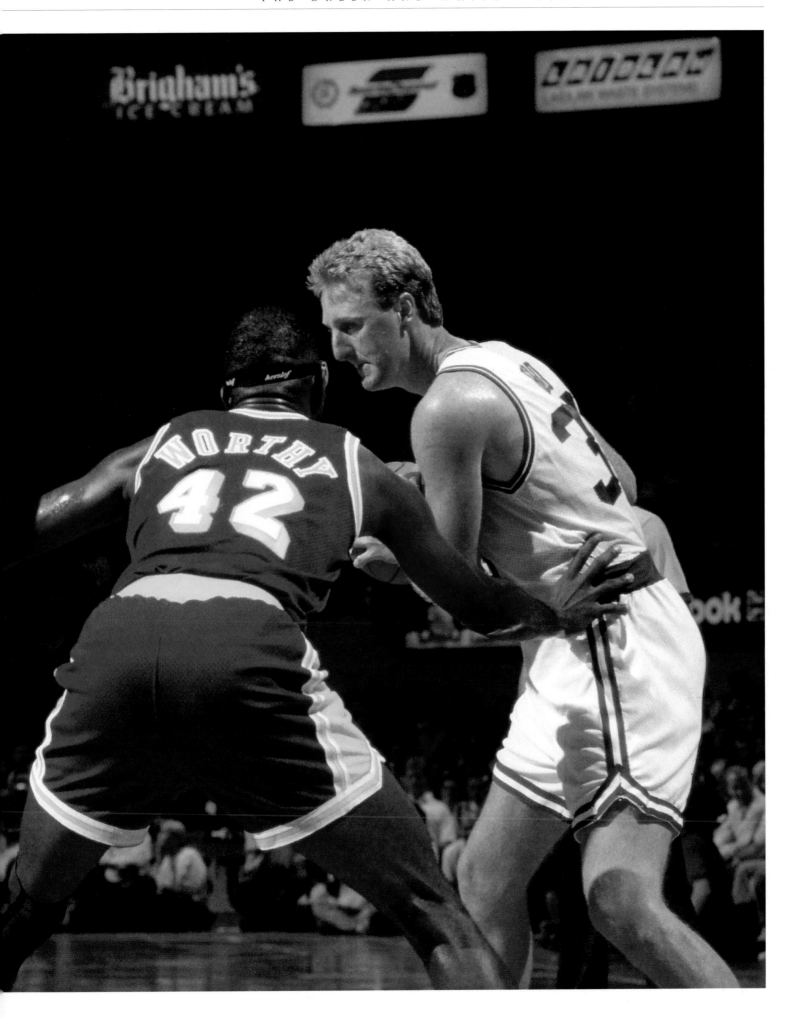

A *playing member of the 1980–81 championship team, Chris Ford, below, was the first player in NBA history to make a three-point shot. He was the Celtics' first player to convert a four-point play. Ford served as head coach for five seasons beginning in 1990–91. His teams went 222-188 and made the playoffs four times. One of his 1994–95 regulars was the high-flying David Wesley (4).*

so was Rodgers—replaced by assistant Chris Ford, the sixth alumnus to coach the Green.

The 1990–91 Celtics responded by winning 56 games while running away with the division by a dozen despite another changing of the guard. Turning 36, Dennis Johnson had retired after seven memorable Boston seasons and was replaced at point guard by Shaw, back from a year's sabbatical in Italy. Shaw teamed with scorer Reggie Lewis in the backcourt, and top draftee Dee Brown contributed as third-guard. And in his third season, Kevin Gamble sprouted and scored a career-high 15.6. The Celtics made it past the playoffs' first round for a change, but not much. After ousting Indiana, 3-2, they took a 2-1 lead over Detroit, then fizzled the next three games.

It was not the best of summers for Bird, who had back surgery before returning for what proved his final season in 1991–92. The back still was menacing him, and Larry missed 37 games—including a month down the stretch while the Celts won 21 of 22 to catch the Knicks at the finish for the Atlantic title. But in a repeat of the previous spring's playoffs, the Celtics got past the miniseries (3-0 over Indiana), then were pasted in the Eastern semifinals (4-3 by Cleveland).

The biggest news would come during the summer. Bird called an August press conference and announced his retirement at age 35—a decision forced by the back misery that had plagued him for years. That ended an era, which began 13 years earlier when the kid from French Lick instantly transformed the Celtics into an exciting, dominating team.

Next it was McHale's turn, playing a final season in 1992–93 as the 48-34 Celtics finished a distant second before being extinguished in the miniseries by Charlotte, 1-3. That abrupt ending got the 35-year-old Minnesotan an earlier start home—his damaged feet and ankles aching from pounding the parquet 13 seasons.

McHale wasn't the only Celtics star to have played a final game. So had Reggie Lewis, who tragically died at 27 after wrapping up a second identical 20.8-point scoring season, his first as captain.

*T*he Boston Garden had its nuances. Above, workers mop water off the parquet after a sudden change in temperature outside and the building's notoriously poor ventilation conspired with the ice below to create a condensation problem that forced a 1990 cancellation. Due to a power failure during the 1988 NHL playoffs, all ushers were required to carry flashlights at subsequent Garden events.

The Celtics said hello to one heavy-duty rebounder, goodbye to another in 1993–94 as the team slid into fifth place at 34-50, 25 games behind, missing the playoffs for the first time in 15 years. Arriving from overseas was 6-foot-11 Croat Dino Radja, a 26-year-old European basketball veteran and two-time silver-medal Olympian who promptly led the Celts in scoring and rebounding. And Parish, the league's oldest player as he approached 41, was moving on to Charlotte—the last survivor of basketball's best frontline, the celebrated Big Three.

M. L. Carr, the charismatic Celtic who had remained in the organization since his Boston playing days of 1979–85, was named executive vice president and director of basketball operations before the 1994–95 season. And after the season he succeeded Chris Ford as coach while retaining his executive roles. Sandwiched between was a mixed bag on and off the court as the Celts played a 49th and final season at the Garden. The Celtics went 20-21 in their Garden farewell, 35-47 overall, sufficient for third place and a playoff berth—before top-seeded Orlando eliminated them.

The Celtics opened the 1995-96 season by moving into the new FleetCenter. A familiar landmark greeted fans: the parquet. The team on the floor was a team that liked to run and shoot. But the Celts finished 33-49, fifth and out of the playoffs. Clearly, it was a time of transition as Carr continued rebuilding as the Celtics enter their second half-century. "This team is solidly on its way back, and I'm excited about it," enthused Carr, encouraged for a variety of reasons, including the addition of blue-chipper Antoine Walker. "We're on the track going in the right direction."

Jan Volk agrees it's more difficult than ever to regenerate from one basketball generation to the next in this era of salary caps and 29 teams drafting. "Celtic success is defined by a different standard than other franchises," Volk said. "People expect more, and we expect more of ourselves in living up to our winning tradition. Anything less is unacceptable." Of course. We're talking *Boston Celtics* here. It's the winning way. ♣

The tradition that began in 1946 was carried onto the relocated parquet at the new FleetCenter for the 1995–96 season by the latest generation of Celtics. The present edition includes forward Eric Williams (55), below, swingman Rick Fox (44) right, and forward Dino Radja (40) far right.

Continuing the legacy left by founder Walter Brown, the Celtics are now led by (from left to right) Executive Vice President and General Manager Jan Volk, President Red Auerbach, Executive Vice President, Director of Basketball Operations, and Head Coach M. L. Carr, and Chairman of the Board Paul Gaston. Gaston has been chairman of the Celtics' parent company, the Boston Celtics Limited Partnership, since 1992. The Gaston family's ownership is second in duration only to that of Brown's, having acquired the team from Harry Mangurian in 1983. In 1986 the Celtics made history by becoming the first sports franchise ever to issue partnership units which are traded on the New York Stock Exchange. At present, there are more than 80,000 unit holders.

Volk began with the Celtics in 1971 as director of ticket sales. He then served as business manager and became the team's legal counsel in 1974. In 1981, he became assistant general manager and was promoted to his present post in 1984. He was a key architect of the 1986 team, which is considered one of the best ever assembled.

FACING PAGE:

It is a feeling, an aura—the green and white warm-ups with the distinctive shamrocks, the sound of ball and shoe against the parquet; the traditional pregame huddle (facing page). The sights, the sounds, the memories . . . the tradition.

CELTISTICS

(1946–47 through 1995–96)

ALL-TIME NUMBERS

1

Never worn by a player.

*Retired in honor of founder Walter Brown

2

Never worn by a player.

*Retired in honor of Coach, President, and General Manager Arnold "Red" Auerbach

3

Mel Hirsch	(1946-47)
Chuck Hoefer	(1946-47—1947-48)
George Nostrand	(1948-49—1949-50)
John Hazen	(1948-49)
	(also wore No. 10)
*Dennis Johnson	(1983-84—1989-90)

4

Wyndol Gray	(1946-47)
Saul Mariaschin	(1947-48)
Tony Lavelli	(1949-50)
	(also wore No. 11)
Sonny Hertzberg	(1949-50—1950-51)
Ken Rollins	(1952-53)
Carl Braun	(1961-62)
Clyde Lovellette	(1962-63—1963-64)
	(also wore No. 34)
Gerry Ward	(1964-65)
Jim Paxson	(1987-88—1989-90)
Larry Robinson	(1991-92)
Sherman Douglas	(1991-92)
	(also wore No. 20)
Alaa Abdelnaby	(1992-93—1993-94)
David Wesley	(1994-95—1995-96)

5

Tony Kappen	(1946-47)
Moe Becker	(1946-47)
Dick Murphy	(1946-47)
Cecil Hankins	(1947-48)
Bill Roberts	(1948-49)
Ed Leede	(1949-50—1950-51)
Lucian (Skip) Whittaker	(1954-55)
John Thompson	(1964-65—1965-66)
	(also wore No. 18)

Bill Walton	(1985-86—1987-88)
John Bagley	(1989-90—1992-93)
Jay Humphries	(1994-95)
Junior Burrough	(1995-96)

6

John Simmons	(1946-47)
George Munroe	(1947-48)
Hank Beenders	(1948-49)
Tom Kelly	(1948-49)
*Bill Russell	(1956-57—1968-69)

7

Warren Fenley	(1946-47)
Mel Riebe	(1947-48—1948-49)
	(also wore No. 9)
Dermie O'Connell	(1948-49—1949-50)
Don Barksdale	(1953-54—1954-55)
	(also wore No. 17)
Emmette Bryant	(1968-69—1969-70)
Art (Hambone) Williams	(1970-71—1973-74)
Ernie DiGregorio	(1977-78)
Nate (Tiny) Archibald	(1978-79—1982-83)
Andre Turner	(1986-87)
Kelvin Upshaw	(1988-89—1989-90)
Dee Brown	(1990-91—1995-96)

8

Al Brightman	(1946-47)
Phil Farbman	(1948-49)
Howie Shannon	(1949-50)
Scott Wedman	(1982-83—1986-87)
	(also wore No. 20)
Kenny Battle	(1991-92—1992-93)
James Blackwell	(1994-95)

9

Harold Kottman	(1946-47)
Mel Riebe	(1947-48—1948-49)
	(also wore No. 7)
George Kaftan	(1948-49)
Al Butler	(1961-62)
Greg Minor	(1994-96)

10

Connie Simmons	(1946-47—1947-48)
Meyer (Mike) Bloom	(1947-48)

Stan Noszka	(1947-48—1948-49)
	(also wore No. 11)
John Hazen	(1948-49)
	(also wore No. 3)
John Ezersky	(1948-49—1949-50)
	(also wore No. 16)
Gene Englund	(1949-50)
Clarence (Kleggie) Hermsen	(1950-51)
*Jo Jo White	(1969-70—1978-79)

11

Kevin (Chuck) Connors	(1946-47—1947-48)
Stan Noszka	(1947-48—1948-49)
	(also wore No. 10)
Chick Halbert	(1948-49)
Tony Lavelli	(1949-50)
	(also wore No. 4)
Chuck Cooper	(1950-51—1953-54)
Mel Counts	(1964-65—1965-66)
Jim Barnett	(1966-67)
Mal Graham	(1967-68—1968-69)
Steve Kuberski	(1969-70—1973-74)
	(also wore No. 33)
Charlie Scott	(1975-76—1977-78)
Bob McAdoo	(1978-79)
Tracy Jackson	(1981-82)
Sam Vincent	(1985-86—1986-87)
Dirk Minniefield	(1987-88)
Michael Smith	(1989-90—1990-91)
Stojko Vrankovic	(1991-92)
	(also wore No. 52)
Dana Barros	(1995-96)

12

Art Spector	(1946-47—1949-50)
Bob Donham	(1950-51—1953-54)
Togo Palazzi	(1954-55—1956-57)
Dan Swartz	(1962-63)
Willie Naulls	(1963-64—1965-66)
Ron Watts	(1965-66—1966-67)
Tom Thacker	(1967-68)
Don Chaney	(1968-69—1974-75, 1977-78—1979-80)
	(also wore No. 42)

ALL-TIME NUMBERS - Continued

Sidney Wicks	(1976-77—1977-78)
Jerry Sichting	(1985-86—1987-88)
Otis Birdsong	(1988-89)
A. J. Wynder	(1990-91)
Kevin Pritchard	(1991-92)
Bart Kofoed	(1992-93)
Chris Corchiani	(1993-94)
Dominique Wilkins	(1994-95)

13

Mike (Red) Wallace	(1946-47)
Gene Stump	(1947-48—1948-49)
Brady Walker	(1949-50—1950-51)
Kenny Sailors	(1950-51)
Dick Mehen	(1950-51)
Bob (Gabby) Harris	(1950-51—1953-54)
	(also wore No. 18)
Charles Smith	(1989-90—1990-91)
Rickey Green	(1991-92)
Todd Day	(1995-96)

14

Don Eliason	(1946-47)
Gerard Kelly	(1946-47)
	(also wore No. 24)
Ed Ehlers	(1947-48—1948-49)
*Bob Cousy	(1950-51—1962-63)

15

Hal Crisler	(1946-47)
Jack (Dutch) Garfinkel	(1946-47—1948-49)
	(also wore No. 21)
Jim Seminoff	(1948-49—1949-50)
Dwight (Red) Morrison	(1954-55—1955-56)
*Tom Heinsohn	(1956-57—1964-65)

16

John Ezersky	(1948-49—1949-50)
	(also wore No. 10)
John Mahnken	(1949-50—1952-53)
Ed Mikan	(1953-54)
Jack Nichols	(1953-54—1957-58)
Ben Swain	(1958-59)
John Richter	(1959-60)
*Tom (Satch) Sanders	(1960-61—1972-73)

17

Virgil Vaughn	(1946-47)
Bob Duffy	(1946-47)
Jack Hewson	(1947-48)
John Janisch	(1947-48)
John Bach	(1948-49)
Joe Mullaney	(1949-50)
Horace (Bones) McKinney	(1950-51—1951-52)
Gene Conley	(1952-53;
	1958-59—1960-61)
Don Barksdale	(1953-54—1954-55)
	(also wore No. 7)
Andy Phillip	(1956-57—1957-58)
*John Havlicek	(1962-63—1977-78)

18

Bob (Gabby) Harris	(1950-51—1953-54)
	(also wore No.13)
Bob Brannum	(1951-52—1954-55)

†Jim Loscutoff	(1955-56—1963-64)
John Thompson	(1964-65—1965-66)
	(also wore No. 5)
Woody Sauldsberry	(1965-66)
Bailey Howell	(1966-67—1969-70)
*Dave Cowens	(1970-71—1979-80)

19

Bob Doll	(1948-49—1949-50)
Ed (Moose) Stanczak	(1950-51)
	(also wore No. 21)
Francis (Mo) Mahoney	(1952-53)
Arnie Risen	(1955-56—1957-58)
Maurice King	(1959-60)
*Don Nelson	(1965-66—1975-76)

20

Al Lucas	(1948-49)
Dick Hemric	(1955-56—1956-57)
Lou Tsioropoulos	(1956-57—1958-59)
	(also wore No.29)
Gene Guarilia	(1959-60—1962-63)
Larry Siegfried	(1963-64—1969-70)
Rex Morgan	(1970-71—1971-72)
Phil Hankinson	(1973-74—1974-75)
Fred Saunders	(1976-77—1977-78)
Wayne Kreklow	(1980-81)
Scott Wedman	(1982-83)
	(also wore No. 8)
Ray Williams	(1984-85)
Darren Daye	(1986-87—1987-88)
Brian Shaw	(1988-89; 1990-91—
	1991-92)
Sherman Douglas	(1991-92—1995-96)
	(also wore No. 4)

21

Jack (Dutch) Garfinkel	(1946-47—1948-49)
	(also wore No.15)
Frank (Apples) Kudelka	(1950-51)
Ed (Moose) Stanczak	(1950-51)
	(also wore No. 19)
Andy Duncan	(1950-51)
*Bill Sharman	(1951-52—1960-61)
Gary Phillips	(1961-62)
Jack (The Shot) Foley	(1962-63)
John McCarthy	(1963-64)
Ron Bonham	(1964-65—1965-66)

22

Ed Sadowski	(1947-48)
Bob Kinney	(1948-49—1949-50)
*Ed Macauley	(1950-51—1955-56)

23

Dick Dickey	(1951-52)
Ernie Barrett	(1953-54—1955-56)
*Frank Ramsey	(1954-55; 1956-57—1963-64)

24

Gerard Kelly	(1946-47)
	(also wore No. 14)
Harry Boykoff	(1950-51)
Fred Scolari	(1954-55)
*Sam Jones	(1957-58—1968-69)

25

*K. C. Jones	(1958-59—1966-67)
	(also wore No. 27)
Enoch (Bud) Olsen	(1968-69)

26

Toby Kimball	(1966-67)
Rick Weitzman	(1967-68)
Rich Johnson	(1968-69—1970-71)
Kermit Washington	(1977-78)

27

K. C. Jones	(1958-59—1966-67)
	(also wore No. 25)
Johnny Jones	(1967-68)
Rich Niemann	(1969-70)
Bill Dinwiddie	(1969-70—1970-71)
Mark Minor	(1972-73)
Kevin Stacom	(1974-75—1977-79)
Marvin Barnes	(1978-79)
Jimmy Oliver	(1993-94)

28

Sihugo Green	(1965-66)
Wayne Embry	(1966-67—1967-68)
Jim (Bad News) Barnes	(1968-69—1969-70)
Willie Williams	(1970-71)
Clarence Glover	(1971-72)
Quinn Buckner	(1982-83—1984-85)

29

Lou Tsioropoulos	(1956-57—1958-59)
	(also wore No.20)
Henry Finkel	(1969-70—1974-75)
Pervis Ellison	(1994-95—1995-96)

30

Glenn McDonald	(1974-75—1975-76)
Cedric Maxwell	(1977-78—1978-79)
	(also wore No.31)
M.L. Carr	(1979-80—1984-85)
Todd Lichti	(1993-94)
Blue Edwards	(1994-95)
Thomas Hamilton	(1995-96)

31

Tom Boswell	(1975-76—1977-78)
Cedric Maxwell	(1977-78—1984-85)
	(also wore No. 30)
Fred Roberts	(1986-87—1987-88)
Ron Grandison	(1988-89)
Xavier McDaniel	(1992-93—1993-94)
Derek Strong	(1994-95)

32

Steve Downing	(1973-74—1974-75)
Ed Searcy	(1975-76)
Jeff Judkins	(1978-79—1979-80)
*Kevin McHale	(1980-81—1992-93)

33

Garfield Smith	(1970-71—1971-72)
Ben Clyde	(1974-75)
Steve Kuberski	(1975-76—1977-78)
	(also wore No. 11)
*Larry Bird	(1979-80—1991-92)

ALL-TIME NUMBERS - Continued

34

Clyde Lovellette	(1962-63—1963-64)
	(also wore No. 4)
Bob Nordmann	(1964-65)
Jim Ard	(1974-75—1976-77)
Bob Bigelow	(1977-78)
Dennis Awtrey	(1978-79)
Rick Carlisle	(1984-85—1986-87)
Kevin Gamble	(1988-89—1993-94)
Xavier McDaniel	(1994-95)
	(also wore No. 31)
Doug Smith	(1995-96)

35

Paul Silas	(1972-73—1975-76)
Tom Barker	(1978-79)
Billy Knight	(1978-79)
Charles Bradley	(1981-82—1982-83)
Sly Williams	(1985-86)
*Reggie Lewis	(1987-88—1992-93)

40

Terry Duerod	(1980-81—1981-82)
Carlos Clark	(1983-84—1984-85)
Dino Radja	(1993-94—1995-96)

41

Curtis Rowe	(1976-77—1978-79)
Tony Massenburg	(1991-92)
Marcus Webb	(1992-93)

42

Don Chaney	(1968-69—1974-75;

	1977-78—1979-80)
	(also wore No. 12)
Jerome Anderson	(1975-76)
Bobby Wilson	(1976-77)
Chris Ford	(1978-79—1981-82)
Mark Acres	(1987-88—1988-89)
Dave Popson	(1990-91)
Joe Wolf	(1992-93)

43

Earl Tatum	(1978-79)
Gerald Henderson	(1979-80—1983-84)
Conner Henry	(1986-87—1987-88)
Derek Smith	(1990-91)
Lorenzo Williams	(1992-93)
Tony Harris	(1993-94—1994-95)

44

Paul Westphal	(1972-73—1974-75)
Dave Bing	(1977-78)
Pete Maravich	(1979-80)
Danny Ainge	(1981-82—1988-89)
Rick Fox	(1991-92—1995-96)

45

Frankie Sanders	(1978-79)
Eric Fernsten	(1979-80—1981-82)
David Thirdkill	(1985-86—1986-87)
Ramon Rivas	(1988-89)
Tony Dawson	(1994-95)

50

Greg Kite	(1983-84—1987-88)

Matt Wenstrom	(1993-94)

51

Charles Claxton	(1995-96)
Todd Mundt	(1995-96)

52

Norm Cook	(1976-77)
Earl Williams	(1978-79)
Darren Tillis	(1982-83)
Stojko Vrankovic	(1990-91)
	(also wore No. 11)

53

Rick Robey	(1978-79—1982-83)
Artis Gilmore	(1987-88)
Joe Kleine	(1988-89—1992-93)
Alton Lister	(1995-96)

54

Zaid Abdul Aziz (Don Smith)	(1977-78)
Brad Lohaus	(1987-88—1988-89)
Ed Pinckney	(1988-89—1993-94)
Larry Sykes	(1995-96)

55

Acie Earl	(1993-94—1994-95)
Eric Williams	(1995-96)

0

Eric Montross	(1994-95—1995-96)

00

Robert Parish	(1980-81—1993-94)

*Number retired in his honor. †Name retired in his honor.

Note: Of the 269 players to have worn a Celtics uniform during a regular-season or playoff game, each one's jersey number has been recorded here except the following (where research has failed): In order of season. Earl Shannon. 5 games, 1948-49; Ward Gibson, 2 games, 1949-50; Bob Houbregs, 2 games, 1954-55. Sometimes the same number was worn by more than one player during a season. Occasionally, for a variety of reasons including lost baggage, a player wore a different number for a game or two. No effort has been made to compile those exceptions.

TEAM LEADERS

(Note: Points per game are based on a minimum of 50 games played)

SEASON	GAMES	MINUTES	FIELD GOALS MADE	FREE THROWS MADE	ASSISTS	REBOUNDS	POINTS	POINTS PER GAME
1946-47	C. Simmons, J. Simmons 60	Unrecorded	C. Simmons 246	C. Simmons 128	C. Simmons 62	Unrecorded	C. Simmons 620	C.Simmons 10.3
1947-48	Riebe, Spector 48	Unrecorded	Sadowski 308	Sadowski 294	Sadowski 74	Unrecorded	Sadowski 910	Sadowski 19.4
1948-49	Ehlers, Spector 59	Unrecorded	Stump 193	Seminoff 151	Seminoff 229	Unrecorded	Ehlers 514	Ehlers 8.7
1949-50	Hertzberg 68	Unrecorded	Hertzberg 275	Leede 223	Seminoff 249	Unrecorded	Hertzberg 693	Kinney 11.1
1950-51	Cousy 69	Unrecorded	Macauley 459	Macauley 466	Cousy 341	Macauley 616	Macauley 1,384	Macauley 20.4
1951-52	Cousy, Macauley, Donham, Cooper, Harris, Brannum 66	Cousy 2,681	Cousy 512	Macauley 496	Cousy 441	Harris 531	Cousy 1,433	Cousy 21.7
1952-53	Cousy, Sharman, Brannum, Donham 71	Cousy 2,945	Cousy 464	Macauley 500	Cousy 547	Macauley 629	Cousy 1,407	Macauley 20.3
1953-54	Cousy 72	Cousy 2,857	Cousy 486	Macauley 420	Cousy 518	Macauley 571	Cousy 1,383	Cousy 19.2
1954-55	Barksdale 72	Cousy 2,747	Cousy 522	Cousy 460	Cousy 557	Macauley 600	Cousy 1,504	Cousy 21.2
1955-56	Sharman, Cousy, Barrett 72	Cousy 2,767	Sharman 538	Cousy 476	Cousy 642	Nichols 625	Sharman 1,434	Sharman 19.9
1956-57	Heinsohn 72	Sharman 2,403	Sharman 516	Sharman 381	Cousy 478	Russell 943	Sharman 1,413	Sharman 21.1
1957-58	Tsioropoulos, Phillip 70	Russell 2,640	Sharman 550	Ramsey 383	Cousy 463	Russell 1,564	Sharman 1,402	Sharman 22.3
1958-59	Sharman, Ramsey 72	Russell 2,979	Sharman 562	Sharman 342	Cousy 557	Russell 1,612	Sharman 1,466	Sharman 20.4
1959-60	Heinsohn, Cousy 75	Russell 3,146	Heinsohn 673	Cousy 319	Cousy 715	Russell 1,778	Heinsohn 1,629	Heinsohn 21.7
1960-61	Ramsey 79	Russell 3,458	Heinsohn 627	Cousy 352	Cousy 587	Russell 1,868	Heinsohn 1,579	Heinsohn 21.3
1961-62	Sanders, K. C. Jones 80	Russell 3,433	Heinsohn 692	Heinsohn 358	Cousy 584	Russell 1,790	Heinsohn 1,742	Heinsohn 22.1
1962-63	Havlicek, Sanders 80	Russell 3,500	Sam Jones 621	Heinsohn 340	Cousy 515	Russell 1,843	Sam Jones 1,499	Sam Jones 19.7
1963-64	Havlicek, Sanders, K. C. Jones 80	Russell 3,482	Havlicek 640	Havlicek 315	K. C. Jones 407	Russell 1,930	Havlicek 1,595	Havlicek 19.9
1964-65	Sam Jones, Sanders 80	Russell 3,466	Sam Jones 821	Sam Jones 428	K. C. Jones 437	Russell 1,878	Sam Jones 2,070	Sam Jones 25.9
1965-66	K. C. Jones 80	Russell 3,386	Sam Jones 626	Sam Jones 325	K. C. Jones 503	Russell 1,779	Sam Jones 1,577	Sam Jones 23.5
1966-67	Havlicek, Howell, Russell Sanders 81	Russell 3,297	Havlicek 684	Havlicek 365	Russell 472	Russell 1,700	Havlicek 1,733	Havlicek 21.4

TEAM LEADERS - Continued

SEASON	GAMES	MINUTES	FIELD GOALS MADE	FREE THROWS MADE	ASSISTS	REBOUNDS	POINTS	POINTS PER GAME
1967-68	Havlicek, Howell, Nelson 82	Russell 2,958	Havlicek 666	Havlicek 368	Havlicek 384	Russell 1,451	Havlicek 1,700	Sam Jones 21.3
1968-69	Havlicek, Sanders, Nelson 82	Russell 3,291	Havlicek 692	Havlicek 387	Havlicek 441	Russell 1,484	Havlicek 1,771	Havlicek 21.6
1969-70	Nelson, Howell 82	Havlicek 3,369	Havlicek 736	Havlicek 488	Havlicek 550	Havlicek 635	Havlicek 1,960	Havlicek 24.2
1970-71	Kuberski, Nelson 82	Havlicek 3,678	Havlicek 892	Havlicek 554	Havlicek 607	Cowens 1,216	Havlicek 2,338	Havlicek 28.9
1971-72	Havlicek, Sanders, Nelson 82	Havlicek 3,698	Havlicek 897	Havlicek 458	Havlicek 614	Cowens 1,203	Havlicek 2,252	Havlicek 27.5
1972-73	Cowens, White 82	Cowens 3,425	Havlicek 766	Havlicek 370	Havlicek 529	Cowens 1,329	Havlicek 1,902	Havlicek 23.8
1973-74	White, Silas, Nelson, Westphal 82	Cowens 3,352	Havlicek 685	Havlicek 346	White 448	Cowens 1,257	Havlicek 1,716	Havlicek 22.6
1974-75	Havlicek, White, Silas, Westphal, Chaney 82	White 3,220	White 658	Havlicek 289	White 458	Silas 1,025	Havlicek 1,573	Cowens 20.4
1975-76	White, Scott 82	White 3,257	White 670	Havlicek 281	White 445	Cowens 1,246	Whites 1,552	Cowens 19.0
1976-77	White, Wicks 82	White 3,333	White 638	White 333	White 492	Wicks 824	White 1,609	White 19.6
1977-78	Havlicek 82	Cowens 3,215	Cowens 598	Bing 244	Cowens 351	Cowens 1,078	Cowens 1,435	Cowens 18.6
1978-79	Judkins 81	Maxwell 2,969	Ford 525	Maxwell 574	Ford 369	Maxwell 791	Maxwell 1,518	Maxwell 19.0
1979-80	Bird, Robey, Carr 82	Bird 2,955	Bird 693	Maxwell 436	Archibald 671	Bird 852	Bird 1,745	Bird 21.3
1980-81	Bird, Parish, McHale, Robey, Parish, Henderson 82	Bird 3,239	Bird 719	Maxwell 352	Archibald 618	Bird 895	Bird 1,741	Bird 21.2
1981-82	Maxwell, Henderson 82	Bird 2,923	Bird 711	Maxwell 357	Archibald 541	Parish 866	Bird 1,761	Bird 22.9
1982-83	McHale, Henderson 82	Bird 2,982	Bird 747	Bird 351	Bird 458	Bird 870	Bird 1,867	Bird 23.6
1983-84	McHale 82	Bird 3,028	Bird 758	Bird 374	Bird 520	Parish 857	Bird 1,908	Bird 24.2
1984-85	Bird, Johnson 80	Bird 3,161	Bird 918	Bird 403	Johnson 543	Bird 842	Bird 2,295	Bird 28.7
1985-86	Bird, Sichting 82	Bird 3,113	Bird 796	Bird 441	Bird 557	Bird 805	Bird 2,115	Bird 25.8
1986-87	Parish 80	McHale 3,060	McHale 790	McHale 428	Johnson 594	Parish 851	Bird 2,076	Bird 28.1
1987-88	Ainge 81	Ainge 3,018	Bird 881	Bird 415	Johnson 598	Bird 703	Bird 2,275	Bird 29.9
1988-89	Shaw 82	McHale 2,876	McHale 661	McHale 436	Johnson, Shaw 472	Parish 996	McHale 1,758	McHale 22.5
1989-90	McHale 82	Bird 2,944	Bird 718	McHale 393	Bird 562	Parish 796	Bird 1,820	Bird 24.3
1990-91	Gamble, Brown 82	Lewis 2,878	Lewis 598	Lewis 281	Shaw 602	Parish 856	Lewis 1,478	Bird 19.4
1991-92	Gamble, Lewis 82	Lewis 3,070	Lewis 703	Lewis 292	Bagley 480	Parish 705	Lewis 1,703	Lewis 20.8
1992-93	Gamble, McDaniel 82	Lewis 3,144	Lews 663	Lewis 326	Douglas 508	Parish 740	Lewis 1,666	Lewis 20.8
1993-94	McDaniel, Fox 82	Brown 2,867	Radja 491	Radja 226	Douglas 683	Radja 577	Radja 1,208	Brown 15.5
1994-95	Brown 79	Brown 2,792	Wilkins 496	Wilkins 266	Douglas 446	Radja 573	Wilkins 1,370	Wilkins 17.8
1995-96	Wesley 82	Fox 2,588	Radja 426	Wesley 217	Wesley 390	Radja 522	Fox 1,137	Radja 19.7

CAREER LEADERS

GAMES		FREE THROWS ATTEMPTED	
1 John Havlicek	1,270	1 John Havlicek	6,589
2 Robert Parish	1,106	2 Bob Cousy	5,753
3 Kevin McHale	971	3 Bill Russell	5,614
4 Bill Russell	963	4 Kevin McHale	4,554
5 Bob Cousy	917	5 Robert Parish	4,491
6 Tom Sanders	916	6 Larry Bird	4,471
7 Larry Bird	897	7 Sam Jones	3,572
8 Don Nelson	872	8 Ed Macauley	3,518
9 Sam Jones	871	9 Cedric Maxwell	3,496
10 Dave Cowens	726	10 Bill Sharman	3,451

POINTS		FREE-THROW PERCENTAGE (1,500 ATTEMPTS)	
1 John Havlicek	26,395	1 Larry Bird	886 (3,960-4,471)
2 Larry Bird	21,791	2 Bill Sharman	883 (3,047-3,451)
3 Robert Parish	18,245	3 Larry Siegfried	855 (1,500-1,755)
4 Kevin McHale	17,335	4 Dennis Johnson	840 (1,527-1,817)
5 Bob Cousy	16,955	5 Jo Jo White	833 (1,892-2,270)
6 Sam Jones	15,411	6 Reggie Lewis	824 (1,479-1,794)
7 Bill Russell	14,522	7 John Havlicek	815 (5,369-6,589)
8 Dave Cowens	13,192	8 Frank Ramsey	804 (2,480-3,083)
9 Jo Jo White	13,188	9 Bob Cousy	803 (4,621-5,753)
10 Bill Sharman	12,287	10 Sam Jones	803 (2,869-3,572)

MINUTES		FREE THROWS MADE		AVERAGE POINTS (3 YRS. MIN.)		ASSISTS	
1 John Havlicek	46,471	1 John Havlicek	5,369	1 Larry Bird	24.3	1 Bob Cousy	6,945
2 Bill Russell	40,726	2 Bob Cousy	4,621	2 John Havlicek	20.8	2 John Havlicek	6,114
3 Robert Parish	34,977	3 Larry Bird	3,960	3 Ed Macauley	18.9	3 Larry Bird	5,695
4 Larry Bird	34,443	4 Kevin McHale	3,634	4 Tom Heinsohn	18.6	4 Bill Russell	4,100
5 Bob Cousy	30,131	5 Robert Parish	3,279	5 Bob Cousy	18.5	5 Jo Jo White	3,686
6 Kevin McHale	30,118	6 Bill Russell	3,148	6 Jo Jo White	18.3	6 Dennis Johnson	3,486
7 Dave Cowens	28,551	7 Bill Sharman	3,047	7 Dave Cowens	18.2	7 K. C. Jones	2,904
8 Jo Jo White	26,770	8 Sam Jones	2,869	8 Bill Sharman	18.1	8 Dave Cowens	2,828
9 Sam Jones	24,285	9 Cedric Maxwell	2,738	9 Bailey Howell	18.0	9 Nate Archibald	2,563
10 Tom Sanders	22,164	10 Ed Macauley	2,724	10 Kevin McHale	17.9	10 Danny Ainge	2,422

CAREER LEADERS - Continued

FIELD GOALS ATTEMPTED

1	John Havlicek	23,930
2	Larry Bird	17,334
3	Bob Cousy	16,465
4	Sam Jones	13,745
5	Robert Parish	13,558
6	Bill Russell	12,930
7	Jo Jo White	12,782
8	Kevin McHale	12,334
9	Dave Cowens	12,193
10	Tom Heinsohn	11,787

FIELD GOALS MADE

1	John Havlicek	10,513
2	Larry Bird	8,591
3	Robert Parish	7,483
4	Kevin McHale	6,830
5	Sam Jones	6,271
6	Bob Cousy	6,167
7	Bill Russell	5,687
8	Jo Jo White	5,648
9	Dave Cowens	5,608
10	Tom Heinsohn	4,773

FIELD GOAL PERCENTAGE (2,000 ATTEMPTS)

1	Cedric Maxwell	559 (2,786-4,984)
2	Kevin McHale	554 (6,830-12,334)
3	Robert Parish	552 (7,483-13,558)
4	Kevin Gamble	518 (2,067-3,988)
5	Rick Robey	510 (1,144-2,241)
6	Larry Bird	496 (8,591-17,334)
7	Gerald Henderson	489 (1,467-3,002)
8	Reggie Lewis	488 (3,198-6,550)
9	Danny Ainge	487 (2,537-5,210)
10	Don Nelson	484 (3,717-7,672)

REBOUNDS

1	Bill Russell	21,620
2	Robert Parish	11,051
3	Dave Cowens	10,170
4	Larry Bird	8,974
5	John Havlicek	8,007
6	Kevin McHale	7,122
7	Tom Sanders	5,798
8	Tom Heinsohn	5,749
9	Bob Cousy	4,781
10	Don Nelson	4,517

PERSONAL FOULS

1	John Havlicek	3,281
2	Robert Parish	3,125
3	Tom Sanders	3,044
4	Dave Cowens	2,783
5	Kevin McHale	2,758
6	Bill Russell	2,592
7	Tom Heinsohn	2,454
8	Larry Bird	2,279
9	Bob Cousy	2,231
10	Frank Ramsey	2,158

DISQUALIFICATIONS

1	Tom Sanders	94
2	Frank Ramsey	87
3	Dave Cowens	86
4	Tom Heinsohn	58
5	Robert Parish	53
6	Bob Brannum	42
7	Don Chaney	40
8	Jim Loscutoff	40
9	Cedric Maxwell	32
10	Bob Donham	31

CELTICS ON ALL-NBA TEAMS

PLAYER	1ST	2ND	3RD	TOTAL
Bob Cousy	10	2	0	12
John Havlicek	4	7	0	11
Bill Russell	3	8	0	11
Larry Bird	9	1	0	10
Bill Sharman	4	3	0	7
Ed Macauley	3	1	0	4
Tom Heinsohn	0	4	0	4
Dave Cowens	0	3	0	3
Sam Jones	0	3	0	3
Jo Jo White	0	2	0	2
Robert Parish	0	1	1	2
Kevin McHale	1	0	0	1
Ed Sadowski	1	0	0	1
Nate Archibald	0	1	0	1

INDIVIDUAL AWARDS

NBA EXECUTIVE OF THE YEAR
(Originated in 1972-73; selected by NBA executives)

1979-80	Red Auerbach

NBA COACH OF THE YEAR
(Originated in 1962-63; selected by the media)

1964-65	Red Auerbach
1972-73	Tom Heinsohn
1979-80	Bill Fitch

NBA MOST VALUABLE PLAYER
(Originated in 1955-56; selected by NBA players)

1956-57	Bob Cousy
1957-58	Bill Russell
1960-61	Bill Russell
1961-62	Bill Russell
1962-63	Bill Russell
1964-65	Bill Russell
1972-73	Dave Cowens
1983-84	Larry Bird
1984-85	Larry Bird
1985-86	Larry Bird

NBA FINALS MOST VALUABLE PLAYER
(Originated in 1969; selected by Sport Magazine)

1974	John Havlicek
1976	Jo Jo White
1981	Cedric Maxwell
1984	Larry Bird
1986	Larry Bird

CELTICS ON NBA'S 35TH ANNIVERSARY TEAM
(Chosen in 1980 to honor the top performers in the league's first 35 seasons.)

Coach:	Red Auerbach
Players:	Bob Cousy
	John Havlicek
	Bill Russell*

* Russell voted the league's greatest all-time player. (In all 11 players were chosen. The other eight: Kareem Abdul-Jabbar, Elgin Baylor, Wilt Chamberlain, Julius Erving, George Mikan, Bob Pettit, Oscar Robertson and Jerry West.)

CELTICS ON NBA'S SILVER ANNIVERSARY TEAM
(Chosen in 1971 to honor the top performers in the league's first 25 seasons.)

Coach	Red Auerbach
Players:	Bob Cousy
	Bill Russell
	Bill Sharman
	Sam Jones

(In all, 10 players were chosen. The other six: George Mikan, Bob Pettit, Dolph Schayes, Paul Arizin, Bob Davies, and Joe Fulks.)

NBA ROOKIE OF THE YEAR
(Originated in 1952-53; selected by the media)

1956-57	Tom Heinsohn
1970-71	Dave Cowens
	(shared with Portland's Geoff Petrie)
1979-80	Larry Bird